Anything Dr. Rod Parsley writes should be required reading for the body of Christ. *Gone* is extraordinary.

—KENNETH COPELAND
KENNETH COPELAND MINISTRIES

It is one thing for us to understand Christ's death from a twenty-first-century perspective, but it was quite another thing for them to view it live in the first century and see their Lord and Savior put into a tomb. In *Gone* Dr. Rod Parsley transports his readers back to the first century, and through facts, history, and traditions lets us walk through the most momentous event in the history of the world in a way we will never forget. It's a must-read you will not regret.

—MARCUS D. LAMB
FOUNDER AND PRESIDENT, DAYSTAR TELEVISION NETWORK

Compelling stories fill Dr. Rod Parsley's latest book, *Gone*, and as he weaves in great illustrations from modern-day life with the power of the resurrection of Christ, the reader is reminded of the single event that didn't just change history, but also defined it. In the style that has made his pulpit ministry so influential, Dr. Parsley will keep your undivided attention, and you will be blessed!

—MIKE HUCKABEE
NEW YORK TIMES BEST-SELLING AUTHOR
FORMER TELEVISION AND RADIO HOST

Most of us know that Jesus's resurrection changed everything, but have you ever looked into all the details surrounding those three days? In *Gone* Rod Parsley explores the history of the resurrection, from the Garden of Gethsemane to the empty tomb, in a way that I think will transform your life.

—ROBERT MORRIS
FOUNDING SENIOR PASTOR, GATEWAY CHURCH
BEST-SELLING AUTHOR, *THE BLESSED LIFE*,
FROM DREAM TO DESTINY, AND *TRULY FREE*

Once again Dr. Rod Parsley has penned a masterpiece of a book in *Gone*. This may be the most detailed book taking the reader on a journey through the most important three days of world history. Christ Himself said that if He be lifted up, He would draw all men unto Him. In my own ministry I have observed that the greatest anointing and altar services always occur after preaching on the subject of Jesus Christ—His life, death, burial, and resurrection. Be prepared to take a journey when reading this book that will clearly paint images of events that changed the world.

—Dr. Perry Stone
Founder, Voice of Evangelism/Perry Stone Ministries

As a former closer for the New York Yankees I know first-hand the importance of finishing off your opponent. Dr. Rod Parsley's description of how Jesus Christ saved humanity by triumphantly closing and sealing our victory through the power of His resurrection is a must-read for all!

—Mariano Rivera
Former New York Yankee
Founder, Mariano Rivera Foundation

Dr. Rod Parsley puts his best foot forward in *Gone* as he weaves snippets of modern history with intricate details of the resurrection weekend in order to paint a newly relevant picture of Christ. So much of what we claim to know and love of the death and resurrection of our Lord is deepened as Dr. Parsley saturates the reader with scriptural facts and challenges. *Gone* challenged me to examine my own interpretation of the crucifixion, death, burial, and resurrection in a way that was enlightening, casting a new light on Christ's redemption plan.

—Dr. Mark L. Williams
Presiding Bishop, Church of God

Dr. Rod Parsley's book *Gone* will change your life! It's like honey flowing from heaven straight from his heart. Read it and you too will fall at the feet of a ready writer.

—JAN CROUCH
PRESIDENT, TBN

In *Gone* Dr. Parsley skillfully paints a portrait of the three most important days in history, weaving the individual perspectives of those involved together with rich insights from Scripture and history, like the many threads of a beautiful tapestry. I found myself entering into their stories and experiencing the resurrection as never before—a truly edifying and inspiring read.

—EVANGELIST DANIEL KOLENDA
PRESIDENT, CHRIST FOR ALL NATIONS

Today we must know 1) what we believe and 2) why we believe it. Rod Parsley's new exciting book, *Gone*, answers both! Jesus uttered from the cross: "It is finished!" He was reporting back to His Holy Father, "Mission accomplished." Total, complete victory over sin, death, hell, and the grave was won. This victory brought fallen man back to God and sealed Satan's doom—once and for all! Jesus defeated Satan at Calvary, and He did it all for you and me. *Gone* is fact-based on the infallible Word of God, and it is a book you will want to read and reread for years to come.

—DWIGHT THOMPSON
DWIGHT THOMPSON MINISTRIES

Dr. Rod Parsley in *Gone* takes us on a powerful journey of the greatest story of love, sacrifice, and redemption. He uses powerful, heartwarming illustrations of events from today to help bring truth, life, and a clearer understanding of the resurrection and power of our Lord and Savior, Jesus Christ! This book is truly a phenomenal read!

—Dr. Fred Hammond
International Recording Artist and Minister

Rod Parsley has penned a classic theatrical of the resurrection of Jesus Christ in his new book, *Gone*. Written in a lyrical style this writing shouts victory to all who will embrace its truths! It is a wonderful companion volume to Dr. Parsley's book *The Cross*. I commend it to all who desire "the power of His resurrection" in their lives.

—Dr. Ron Phillips
Senior Pastor, Abba's House

The age-old story of the resurrection of Jesus Christ of Nazareth comes to life in this brilliant portrayal by Dr. Rod Parsley. Believers across the globe know that Jesus was crucified, died, and rose again, but few have ever fully explored the mystery of exactly where He was during those three days in the tomb. I invite you to take a compelling journey into the depth of this powerful successor to *The Cross*.

—Sheryl Brady
Pastor, The Potter's House of North Dallas

Dr. Rod Parsley has done it again in his new literary work, *Gone*. For more than forty years he's been on the frontline, upholding the blood-stained banner of the Lord and proclaiming righteousness to this generation. And here he does it again powerfully, walking readers through the rights and privileges of every believer. As you read *Gone*, you'll gain a deep understanding that death is not the final frontier—for if Christ be in you, He is the hope of glory! Now is the time for believers to respond to the clarion call to rise up and walk into the enemy's camp. This book will give you the right and the tools to take your heel and press it against the head of the serpent so that you can walk in victory, breakthrough, and deliverance. It has changed my life. I am certain it is going to change yours too.

—BISHOP GEORGE G. BLOOMER
SENIOR PASTOR, BETHEL FAMILY WORSHIP CENTER

When Rod Parsley talks, the world listens. When Rod Parsley talks, I change. This book of wisdom will change *you* forever. Invest in copies as gifts to significant friends. Thank you, mentor and man of God, for your spectacular investment in all of us!

—DR. MIKE MURDOCK
FOUNDER, THE WISDOM CENTER

I consider it an honor and a privilege to write an endorsement for my friend Dr. Rod Parsley for any one of his anointed books; however, this one is of particular importance to the body of Christ. *Gone* deals with the most imperative message of all times—Jesus is alive! The resurrection of Jesus is the basis for our salvation, redemption, provision, healing, deliverance, and more. Indeed, it is "the jubilee of the universe," as Dr. Parsley coins it for all who would confess Jesus as Lord. In this book Dr. Parsley goes on to explain this message with powerful revelation and a solid biblical base in such a way that it will bless and impact people in this and other countries, spanning various cultures, ethnicities, and age groups. This message is for everyone! Therefore, I strongly encourage you, whether you are a pastor, leader, or church member, to read Dr. Parsley's latest book, *Gone*, because its central message— the resurrection of Jesus—has the power to renew your soul, transform your mind, mobilize you in your calling, and completely revolutionize your life!

—APOSTLE GUILLERMO MALDONADO
FOUNDING SENIOR PASTOR, KING JESUS INTERNATIONAL
MINISTRY

Rod Parsley has done it again! A prolific author, with an end-times call to holiness and the altar, Dr. Parsley has once again written a powerful evangelism tool for the body of Christ. *Gone* will change your life forever. It is a must-read for every Christian. I pray everyone everywhere will read this book and be enlightened and inspired to chase God and enjoy the full benefits of Calvary. This is the best book I've ever read on this critical subject. I hold the author in high esteem. Great job, Rod!

—Dr. Mark T. Barclay
President, Supernatural Ministries Training Institute
President, Righteous Preachers' Network
Founder, Living Word International Church

Rod Parsley is a phenomenal pastor, teacher, and author. This new book contains powerful insights and biblical revelation that bring to life the power of Jesus and His resurrection! That power is still with us today. For those looking for an in-depth study of the biblical, historical, and spiritual meaning of the crucifixion, death, and resurrection power of Jesus Christ this book is a must-read. The revelations in this book are dynamic and will change your life forever!

—Larry Huch
Senior Pastor, New Beginnings Church

Without an empty tomb we all were certainly doomed! Rod Parsley's latest release, *Gone*, is absolutely riveting, thought provoking, incredibly insightful, and powerful. Death and shame have no power over us because Jesus, our hero, conquered the grave. Reading this book will revolutionize your life!

—Dr. Medina Pullings
United Nations Church International

The capstone principle upon which Christianity stands is the doctrine of Christ. Failure to align with this biblical doctrine—especially the truth of Christ's resurrection—lies at the root of most heretical deviations from true faith. Rod Parsley, in *Gone*, utilizes his deep understanding of Scripture and his access to the latest findings of responsible scholarship to make a rock-solid defense for this crucial doctrine. Parsley goes beyond the cold facts of research and presents a warm, personal, you-are-there portrayal of the events of the Sunday that changed the world.

—Dr. T. L. Lowery
T. L. Lowery Global Foundation

Reading this book was like a living adventure! The emotions of my soul embraced the horrifying challenges of a prisoner of war. Eloquent words from the author's pen carried me to a bleeding hill of the suffering Christ. As my heart felt the cold dark shadows of night, the clouds rolled back, and I began to soar as an eagle with resurrection power. It's all about Jesus, and it just doesn't get any better than that.

—Tommy Bates
Senior Pastor, Community Family Church

Dr. Rod Parsley does it again in his new book, *Gone*. For an emerging and new generation of believers this book will radically and fundamentally change the way they view the relevance and significance of the death, burial, and resurrection of Christ. I predict they will be encouraged to live a life pleasing to God in an anti-Christ world. For the mature saint, this book underscores the Apostle Paul's statement, "For to me to live is Christ, and to die is gain" (Phil. 1:21, KJV). It is my prayer that each reader will see the passion of Christ and resolve within their hearts that anything we do for God is not only worth living for, it is also worth dying for.

—Dr. N. Cindy Trimm
Author, Minister, Life Strategist

Dr. Rod Parsley is a mighty leader in the kingdom, a most remarkable man of God. This book is a must-read for all God's people. The anointing of seven times greater will be sensed as you read this power-packed book. Dr. Parsley is a great friend, as well as an on-point prophetic voice, powerful pastor and author. If you read one book in 2016, this is it!

—Dr. Coy Barker
Author and Senior Pastor, Elevation Point Church

In this thought-provoking book Rod Parsley takes us on a journey full of insight and revelation that opens the eyes of the reader and shows that what looks like earth's and heaven's darkest day is really its most triumphant!

—Darlene Bishop
Solid Rock Church

I'm never surprised at how Rod Parsley, the amazing preacher and teacher that he is, so masterfully expounds on the Word of God. In *Gone* Rod has done it again! In it he asks: "What made the Resurrection the linchpin of God's grand design to wrest control of the earth away from that ancient deceiver? Why did divine justice demand not only the death of an unblemished innocent but also the conquest of the grave? What really transpired in those hours between that late Passover Friday afternoon and that Sunday morning?"

I agree with Rod that if the church were to truly grasp the answers to these questions, if the eyes of our understanding were opened to what really happened that weekend and what one man, in one tomb, on one Sunday accomplished for us, it would transform everything in us and around us. I believe God's anointing is on Rod Parsley to hear from Him and communicate the truth of His Word in such a way that the eyes of our understanding are truly opened. This book, and the revelation it brings about Jesus's death, burial, and resurrection, is proof of that. Not only will it change how you view the Resurrection, but it will also change your life!

—HENRY FERNANDEZ
SENIOR PASTOR, THE FAITH CENTER

There probably isn't a biblical verse that better depicts ultimate defeat more than, "O death, where is thy sting? O grave, where is thy victory?" (1 Cor. 15:55, KJV). This taunting phrase makes a mockery of hell's evil intent with the joyous reminder that death and the grave do not get the final word. Death has been utterly beaten by One who disappeared from a guarded tomb. Once again Rod Parsley has constructed a masterful literary work. In poetic, story-like form, coupled with sound biblical truth and historical accuracy, Dr. Parsley skillfully details the magnificent impact of Jesus's empty grave upon humanity. His book *Gone* is a captivating writing that is easily grasped by the newest believer, but it is saturated with in-depth revelation that influences the most mature saint. It is a must-read for every person who desires to understand and truly know the power of the Resurrection!

—HANK AND BRENDA KUNNEMAN
ONE VOICE MINISTRIES AND LORD OF HOSTS CHURCH

Dr. Parsley once again delivers an instant classic as he expounds on the intricacies of the greatest event ever recorded in human history, the resurrection of our Savior. This book will be referenced for generations.

—PASTOR MARK VEGA
MARK VEGA EVANGELISTIC MINISTRIES

Dr. Rod Parsley's message is a rhema word on the suffering, death, and resurrection of our Savior. It delivers the reader from having spiritual selective memory during difficult times in their lives. The words on the pages of this book ignite new levels of faith and proclaim that the promises of the Lord are *yes* and *amen*, even in the midst of experiences between Christ's crucifixion and resurrection.

—KIMBERLY DANIELS
SPOKEN WORD MINISTRIES

Pastor Parsley's book *Gone* is an enchanting story that will captivate you from the very beginning. Utilizing famous historical events, he is able to set a scene that is parallel to the happenings of Jesus. *Gone* explores the mysteries of Christ's resurrection and exposes the truth about privities from the time Jesus was placed in the tomb until the time He rose. In reading this book, you will change the manner in which you think, worship, believe, expect, experience, and witness. If you are ready to ascend to the next level, it is imperative that you read this book. It will change your life forever.

—BISHOP ORRIN PULLINGS
UNITED NATIONS CHURCH INTERNATIONAL

In this masterpiece book *Gone* Dr. Rod Parsley has brilliantly, dynamically, and passionately captured the eternal revelation of the most important and significant event and story since Creation: Jesus's life, death, burial, and supernatural resurrection. This book will take the body of Christ to a whole new level of revelation about Jesus Christ our Savior.

—DR. FRANK SUMMERFIELD
FOUNDER AND SENIOR PASTOR, WORD OF GOD FELLOWSHIP
CHURCH

In his latest book, *Gone*, with riveting clarity Dr. Rod Parsley unfolds the events revolving around the resurrection of the King of the ages, Jesus Christ. Every hope-filled, death-defeating page encourages the reader to embrace the crown jewel of Christianity's faith, a risen Savior, a ransomed bride, and an empty tomb.

—JIM RALEY
AUTHOR AND LEAD PASTOR, CALVARY CHRISTIAN CENTER
ORMOND BEACH, FLORIDA
PRESIDENT AND FOUNDER, CALVARY NETWORK
INTERNATIONAL

Dr. Parsley, one of our generation's foremost and greatest proponents of the Cross, has now turned our attention to the Resurrection. The Resurrection is not just an event. It is a revelation. One, which if received, will revolutionize every area of our faith and Christian walk. *Gone* is a timeless masterpiece with a message that is vital for today. No matter who you are, your call, or your occupation, *Gone* will indeed revolutionize your life as you experience the event and the revelation of Christ's resurrection.

—JONATHAN MILLER
PASTOR, NEW BEGINNINGS HEALING CENTER

In *Gone* Dr. Rod Parsley challenges even the most seasoned of Christians to analyze and reconcile hard but real truths, including those not fully exposed in the Bible regarding the circumstances immediately following Jesus's death on that dark Friday. What really happened during the waiting period throughout the entire day on that silent Saturday and the glorious resurrection events on liberty Sunday? This is a must-read for those who seek a solid faith foundation, those who seek to build upon their faith foundation, or those who simply seek truth about the greatest love story of all time. This second installment in the trilogy begun with *The Cross* will continue to transform the lives of those who seek to grow in every way as they continue their spiritual journey in a time-space

continuum that so easily causes us to lose focus on the significance of the Cross to each and every life potential.
—Bishop John I. Cline
Author and Pastor, New Life Baptist Church

Dr. Rod Parsley has done it again. Without question, he is a gifted writer. I was captivated from the first few paragraphs of *Gone* and didn't want to put it down. I found myself wanting to read more. I believe this new contribution will bring hope and life to multiplied thousands of believers around the world. I was personally blessed and encouraged by this book, and I know you will be too.
—David Binion
Worship Pastor, Covenant Church
Carrollton, Texas

Never before has there been a greater need for the message of *Gone* by Dr. Rod Parsley. In the midst of despair and the darkest moments of our lives, Parsley reminds us that our purpose was locked in the tomb in Christ and is made available to us through His glorious resurrection! This is a must-read to understand the pain of the tomb and the authority of the Resurrection! Glory to God!
—Trent Cory
International Recording Artist/Minister/Songwriter

GONE

GONE

One Man...
One Tomb...
One Sunday...

ROD PARSLEY

CHARISMA
HOUSE

GONE by Rod Parsley
Published by Charisma House
Charisma Media/Charisma House Book Group
600 Rinehart Road
Lake Mary, Florida 32746
www.charismahouse.com

Cover design by Cameron Fontana
Design Director: Justin Evans

Visit the author's website at www.rodparsley.com.

Library of Congress Control Number: 2016930121
International Standard Book Number: 978-1-62998-934-1 (trade paperback); 978-1-62998-935-8 (hardback)
E-book ISBN: 978-1-62998-936-5

While the author has made every effort to provide accurate Internet addresses at the time of publication, neither the publisher nor the author assumes any responsibility for errors or for changes that occur after publication.

First edition

16 17 18 19 20 — 9 8 7 6 5 4 3 2 1
Printed in the United States of America

DEDICATION

It is a great privilege for me to dedicate this book to my fraternal and maternal grandparents, Allan and Molly (Miller) Parsley and Samuel and Eva (Pack) Endicott. They endured hardships and suffered privations unknown to their grandchildren so that they could provide a better world and way of life for all who followed them.

The inheritance they gave us was not of material things, but of faith and perseverance—of fidelity to God's Word and praise to Him in the face of circumstances that would have silenced and stopped less courageous men and women.

Even though they are gone from this life, they are present in my heart, as well as in the great cloud of witnesses who cheer us on from the grandstands of heaven as we run with patience the race that is set before us. Until we meet again, we who remain here have the promise of a living hope, as the Apostle Peter said—the hope that is born in our hearts concerning a glorious resurrection that was not only proclaimed but also proven by Jesus Christ in His triumph over death, hell, and the grave.

CONTENTS

FOREWORD

I T IS OFTEN said that God has innumerable children but no grandchildren. An inherited faith is an inherently weak faith. So the basic truths of the gospel—the distinctive beliefs that make men and women *Christian*—must be taught in every era and withstand the scrutiny of the self-appointed intellectual elites of that era.

It stands to reason, then, that master teachers of the essentials of our faith must rise in every generation. Andrew Murray was such a man for his generation. Charles Haddon Spurgeon, William Seymour, G. E. Patterson, and E. V. Hill filled the role in subsequent years. With the publication of *Gone*, I believe that my good friend Rod Parsley is continuing to fulfill the role of a great teacher of the Christian faith.

This should come as no surprise to anyone who has studied his sermons in any depth or taken the time to learn about his testimony as an evangelist, television host, humanitarian, statesman, and educator. Over the years he has consistently followed Spurgeon's admonition to "preach with fire and pathos and passion," because nothing less would do for the God that Rod Parsley knows. The source of his shout is unmistakable; it is rooted in a passionate love for Jesus Christ and a deep-rooted knowledge of His Word, the Bible. *Gone* graphically portrays the tragedy of Christ's crucifixion and masterfully explains the marvelous glory of His resurrection.

Like *The Cross* before it, this book is the result of painstaking research. And the fascinating insights Dr. Parsley has uncovered about the Resurrection are expertly communicated in a volume that will enlighten everyone who reads it—from the newest believer to the most seasoned saint.

In reading the book, two things happened for me. First, I discovered a new depth of awe for God's plan. Then, I fell in love with Him all over again. I suspect that's what my friend Rod Parsley had in mind for me—and for you. Enjoy the wisdom and inspiration on the pages that follow. You will come to thoroughly understand and deeply appreciate the fact of the Resurrection, and you will be compelled to live your life in light of what you know about it. That can only lead to profoundly changed congregations, profoundly changed communities, and a profoundly changed church. I encourage you to enjoy and be blessed by this masterful work from the heart of Dr. Rod Parsley. To God be the glory!

—BISHOP CHARLES E. BLAKE SR.
WEST ANGELES COGIC
PRESIDING BISHOP, CHURCH OF GOD IN CHRIST
LOS ANGELES, CALIFORNIA

PART I:

FRIDAY

INTRODUCTION

Why do you seek the living among the dead?
He is not here.

> LUKE 24:5–6

A MAN WHO AT twenty-six years of age has already earned the right to be considered one of the greatest military heroes is sick and starving. He lies exhausted but sleepless on the concrete floor of a tiny jungle prison cell along with nine other US prisoners of war. At six feet, two inches tall, he weighs scarcely one hundred twenty pounds.

For Captain William Dyess, US Army Air Force, the Philippine island of Mindanao is a very long way from home. Home is little Albany, Texas, a few miles outside of Abilene. The pilot has already survived the ordeal that came to be known as the Bataan Death March. This was followed by a year of unspeakably punishing captivity at the hands of the Japanese military. He has watched countless friends and comrades die in the most brutal and shocking ways imaginable.

Dyess is only one of thousands of more-dead-than-alive American, British, and Filipino prisoners suffering unbelievable hardships in Imperial Japan's infamous network of prison camps. What sets him apart is that he *chose* to be here. He could have avoided this, but he refused freedom, allowing another soldier to escape capture in his stead. It was a heroic decision that he made not once, but twice.

It hadn't even been two years since America entered the global conflagration that was World War II. Even so, among the battle-hardened warriors of "the greatest generation," Captain Dyess's exploits as a P-40 Warhawk pilot and his unflinching fearlessness in the face of grave danger were already the makings of a mighty military legend. Lying in that squalid cell racked with pain, he would be astonished to learn that one day an air force base in Abilene would proudly bear his name. On this day, however, Dyess had only two things on his mind. The first was to help himself and his comrades survive another day of hell in the Davao Penal Colony, a prisoner of war (POW) camp. Second, he thought of escaping so the world could learn the deplorable truth about what his fellow servicemen and their allies were brutally suffering as captives in this part of the world. He believed that if the United States military leadership and the American people could be informed of the barbarous and atrocious treatment of Allied prisoners, he might be allowed to lead an effort to rescue all of them before they all succumbed to starvation, disease, and systematic torture.

As background, it's important to understand just how badly the war in the Pacific was going for the United States in order to grasp how truly desperate the situation was in which our honorable servicemen found themselves.

On December 7, 1941, with the sudden and brutal Japanese attack on Pearl Harbor, the United States lost a significant portion of its naval fleet in that half of the world. The blow was designed to cripple America's ability to respond to Japan's true objective: taking control of the entire southeastern Pacific by driving America out of the Philippine Islands. That strategy proved devastatingly effective.

Immediately after the Pearl Harbor attack, the Japanese

invaded the Philippines. Within ten days, Japanese General Masaharu Homma estimated that most of the US Air Force in the region had been destroyed. By January 2, 1942, the Japanese controlled Manila. General Douglas MacArthur, commander of the US Army Forces in the Far East, was forced to withdraw to Australia. When he arrived, he uttered his famous line, "I came through and I shall return."[1] After another week of relentless Japanese advances, Homma had the only remnant of US forces cornered in Bataan, a peninsula of the main island of Luzon.

In Bataan, roughly seventy thousand American troops and twenty-six thousand Filipino civilians were cut off and running out of ammunition, parts, and food. Anything that could be eaten—monkeys, dogs, cavalry horses—was. Even so, it took the Japanese four full months to overrun Bataan. Captain Dyess, commander of the Twenty-First Pursuit Squadron, was a major reason why. His strategic offensive tactics were exceptional, especially considering the dire circumstances surrounding them.

The Americans fought to hold off the Japanese invasion until General MacArthur could "return" as promised with reinforcements. In those desperate weeks, Dyess earned a nickname from his fellow soldiers. They began calling him "The One-Man Scourge." The reason? Almost single-handedly, Dyess attacked and hindered Japanese amphibious landings over and over again. On numerous occasions he cobbled together a functioning P-40 and, aided by a single wingman, attacked Japanese positions. Although weak and malnourished—and often scarcely strong enough to pilot the plane—he sank numerous Japanese vessels and managed to delay the final assault on Bataan, and as a result, ultimately saved thousands of lives.

Finally, massively outnumbered, out of ammunition, starving, and with no remaining options, it became clear that continued resistance was impossible. The remaining forces in Bataan were ordered to evacuate to the island of Corregidor. There was just one problem. There were only enough aircraft to evacuate a fraction of the American servicemen there.

Dyess, highly valued by his superior officers, was ordered to fly his plane off the island immediately, but he simply refused to leave his men and comrades behind. He put another pilot in his plane and sent him to safety instead. Just as the Japanese were about to overrun the base, one final cargo plane arrived to evacuate a few more officers. Again, Dyess defied orders, refusing to leave. He gave his seat on the plane to a Philippine Army colonel named Carlos Rómulo. It was a historic decision. Rómulo would survive the war and go on to become the fourth president of the United Nations General Assembly, the founder of the Boy Scouts of the Philippines, and a university president.

A day later, Dyess became a part of the largest mass surrender in American military history. Tens of thousands of Americans and Filipinos became prisoners of the Japanese Empire. What followed was one of the most infamous and shameful chapters in the history of modern warfare. Without food or water in the blazing heat and humidity of that Philippine island, the already weak and ailing prisoners were ordered to march eighty miles inland. History would ultimately catalog this as the infamous Bataan Death March that began on April 9, 1942.

The horrors and atrocities of that ordeal became synonymous with inhumanity. As the lethal combination of starvation, heat, and dehydration brutally took its toll on the prisoners, the Japanese began executing any who stumbled or fell behind. Dyess was determined to make sure this didn't happen to any of his men. He kept them together and moving forward no matter how sick and weak they became.

Over the course of the next year, Dyess was moved to three different POW camps, each more punishing and dehumanizing than the one before. Finally he arrived at Davao, and it is there that he formulated his plan to escape. He knew that if he did not, he would die. More important to him, thousands of others would also share his fate. He became convinced that if he didn't escape this pit of hopelessness and despair, no one ever would.

On the evening of April 4, 1943, the end-of-day roll call at Davao Penal Colony commenced. Skeletal figures lined up in rows and struggled to stay upright. Heads were counted. They were counted again. There was consternation and agitated chatter among the Japanese guards. Then, there was a hurried third count. Finally a thorough inventory of prisoners revealed the truth. Someone was missing.

It was Captain William Dyess. He had escaped when escape was thought impossible. What is more, he took nine other prisoners with him. Soon the world would know the truth. Dyess put events in motion that would result in the freedom of many more captives.

Still, his cruel captors could not believe what had happened. It was true, all the same. Their prized prisoner was *gone*.

Twenty centuries ago another hero stepped forward to champion the cause of captives by becoming one Himself. He too could have chosen freedom. He too could have escaped the pain. Yet He entered into the suffering of His brothers willingly. He chose the chains. He extended His hands to the shacklers, offered His back to the torturers, and completed the most grueling death march ever undertaken.

His merciless, hate-filled enemy believed he had the valiant Captain of Souls hopelessly and eternally confined to a dark and inescapable prison that millions upon millions had entered across six millennia. Yet one morning, a head count was taken—shock waves reverberated throughout the darkened corridors of the doomed and the damned. The unequaled Hero was no longer in that cold gray stone cell. The Champion of the ages was...gone.

Chapter 1

The JUBILEE of the UNIVERSE

Since the resurrection morning there has never been—there could not be—the slightest question as to His final rulership of the world. Death was conquered, Satan was conquered, and He proclaimed the wearer of the name above every name.[1]

> ➤ E. P. GOODWIN
> (1832–1901)

L OOK BACK WITH me across the long, tortured landscape of human history. With a single sweeping gaze, cast your eye back through millennia of striving, suffering, progress, and pain. View the entirety of the timeline of mankind's sojourn on the earth—across the hills of hope and valleys of despair—and your eye will instantly note two particular geological features standing out more than any others.

First, in the most distant recesses of the ancient past, as you peer back into man's earliest days of dominion over this brilliant blue marble, we discern the outlines of a deep gorge. Look more closely. This dark and seemingly bottomless chasm is filled with regret, shame, and loss. This low point in history's

7

rolling topography represents that awful day mankind's parents traded away the deed to a pristine planet for a bright, shiny lie. It represents the fatal blunder that ushered in the new and terrible era among men—the reign of Death.

Then the eye travels forward through the tear-soaked centuries and is drawn to a solitary peak, towering above the landscape. This soaring summit represents a day—roughly twenty centuries prior to our time—in which a lone and lonely descendant of that first couple ended Death's reign by utterly defeating it. This colossal peak has a name: *Mount Resurrection.*

The other, earlier feature on history's landscape, that yawning abyss of black despair, marks the fall of the first Adam. He and his bride's gullible embrace of a flattering deceiver's slander unleashed a flood of woe and pain upon a perfect world by disobeying the one stipulation their God and Creator had set before them. Grief and sorrow rushed in to fill the vacuum created by the loss of intimate connectedness to God, their loving and compassionate Father. Dominion stewardship over the earth slipped from Adam's grasping fingers. There in that garden paradise, humanity's parents were duped into handing over their God-granted authority and their keys to the kingdom. The terrible and tragic result was the entire earth being placed in relentless subjection to degeneration, decay, and death. The contemptible and cruel curse had commenced. From that day forward, Death reigned victorious over mankind and the once lavish, pristine earth that he had been assigned to rule.

Such is the immense depth of that valley. But that peak—oh, that wonderful mountaintop is as glorious as that abyss is dark. The Resurrection is the zenith of God's extraordinary redemptive strategy to legally restore what had been lawfully forfeited. It marks the consummation of His plan of the ages and the revealing of a mystery hidden since the foundation of the world. That mystery was wrapped up in the sinless life, matchless death, and third-day victory of the Last Adam—our reigning King of kings and Lord of lords, the Lord Jesus Christ.

Mere words stagger and fail under the burden of attempting to encompass the magnitude and glory of this event. Even so, in the words of a great circuit-riding Methodist preacher of the nineteenth century:

> But who is this that cometh from the tomb? He that is glorious in His appearance, walking in the greatness of strength? It is thy Prince, O Zion! Christian, it is your Lord!...He hath stained His raiment with blood; but now as the first-born from the womb of nature, He meets the morning of His resurrection. He arises, a conqueror from the grave; He returns with blessings from the world of spirits; He brings salvation to the sons of men. Never did the returning sun usher in a day so glorious! It was the jubilee of the universe![2]

The jubilee of the universe. This wasn't hyperbole. In Old Testament Israel, God instituted the jubilee year as one in which all debts were canceled, prisoners released, slaves liberated, forfeited property restored, and scattered families reunited. (See Leviticus 25:8–34.) As we're about to discover, these remarkable blessings are all present in abundance at the summit of Mount Resurrection.

The day Jesus vanquished Death, man's greatest foe, represents the apex of God's patient, brilliantly executed, redemptive program. In other words, the event we commonly call *the resurrection* of Jesus Christ is the most significant ever to transpire on this or any other world.

Christians of every creed and culture readily affirm this assertion with a "Yes, amen," yet most would be hard-pressed to explain precisely *why*, or in what *way*. Jesus Christ, the Son of God, was dead and buried, and then He was alive again. "Of course, He's alive," we think. "He was the Son of God!" This is the story of Easter every eight-year-old Sunday schooler knows.

Yes, but what made the Resurrection the linchpin of God's grand design to wrest control of the earth away from that ancient deceiver? Why did divine justice demand not only the death of an unblemished innocent but also the conquest of the grave? What really transpired in those hours between that late Passover Friday afternoon and that Sunday morning? Was the spirit and soul of the Lamb of God sleeping? If not, what unseen drama unfolded in that seemingly silent span between the moment witnesses watched Jesus of Nazareth expel His final labored breath and that extraordinary Sunday morning when He entreated a delirious Mary Magdalene, "Touch me not, for I have not yet ascended to my Father"?

These questions represent profound mysteries to most believers. Our understanding of the Resurrection is a mile wide and a quarter-inch deep.

Were we to truly grasp the answers to these questions—if the eyes of our understanding were opened to what really happened that weekend and what one man, in one tomb, on one Sunday accomplished for us—it would transform everything in us and around us.

It would revolutionize the way we *think* about our lives, turning our priorities upside down and causing us to "leave our nets" (our ideas and agendas) to follow Him, just as the disciples did!

It would change the way we *worship*, moving us to push aside every hindrance and pour out every ounce of adoration and adulation we could muster upon heaven's Crown Prince as we remember and reflect on His furious love toward us and the dear price He paid to redeem us.

It would change the way we *believe*, invigorating our faith and infusing every fiber of our beings with holy boldness. We would tolerate no more status quo Christianity as we flowed in a current that is forever contrary to anything and everything ordinary.

It would change what we *expect*, filling us with confidence that God's mercy and favor flow toward us, and that we are instruments to be used by Him for His glory. We already know that the atmosphere of expectancy is the breeding ground of miracles!

It would change what we *experience*, transforming our lives into ongoing public demonstrations of God's divine power. We would contract a heavenly contagion and become carriers of a communicable disease called Holy Ghost power!

It would change the power of our *witness*, sweeping us into the highways and byways of this sin-sick culture, proclaiming the truth of the gospel with the power to shake whole cities and even entire countries into revival as we lift high the name of Jesus to rescue a generation, restore a nation, and revitalize a civilization.

In other words, I am suggesting that the resurrection of Jesus Christ is not only the apex of redemptive history, it should be the apex of our faith. So we will probe this topic together on the following pages.

Let us begin by looking with fresh eyes at the events leading up to that day of days. Before we can bask in the golden light of that Sunday morning dawn, we must peer into the fading light of Friday. Before we comprehend pure hope, we should stare into the face of hopelessness. Before we can see Christ risen from the tomb, we must first observe Him laid in it.

We must gather our courage and go back to the moment when God was dead.

✝ ✝ ✝ ✝ ✝

In my previous book *The Cross: One Man...One Tree...One Friday...* I explored the depth and breadth of Jesus's sacrificial death on Calvary's cruel, angry, and biting beam. With sadness I pointed to the reality that, for many churches and for the believers who attend them, the cross has lost its rightful place at the center of our preaching and theology. Readers discovered the necessity of the awful price Jesus had to pay to redeem this cursed planet and the souls of men, and why His death had to take place on a cross. I mined the "seven last words of Christ" for riches of meaning and understanding. Together we discovered the astounding truth about just how far the Lamb of God's redemptive work extends in our lives.

That book serves as prelude to this one. Indeed, the Cross and the Resurrection are really two halves of a single genius masterwork of redemptive art. In another sense these events represent Act I and Act II of God's thrilling three-act drama. The final act is yet to be performed, but instead of a curtain-rise, the Prince of Heaven will split the eastern skies with pure glory and might, and with His return, a bridegroom will run into the embrace of His spotless, overcoming bride. We'll explore this final plot twist before our journey is complete.

But first, Act II opens on a scene of unspeakable sorrow. A handful of grief-stricken individuals stare in disbelief and horror at what remains of a man they loved, hanging limp and breathless from a blood-soaked beam.

Over the previous eighteen hours the blameless Son of God has run a vicious spiritual, emotional, and physical gauntlet. It began in the Garden of Gethsemane, where the war of self-will was waged and where the capillaries of His face burst at the thought that He might fall short of accomplishing His Father's will by dying there, having never made it to the cross. He had been arrested and bludgeoned beyond recognition while in custody. He had been mocked, spat upon, insulted, and reviled. Sleepless and dehydrated, He endured an unspeakably violent and grisly scourging by a Roman torturer who expertly wielded a specialized whip called a *flagrum*. The cursed whip consisted of a long wooden handle attached to several strips of leather with a series of stone beads or metal balls spaced periodically along the length of each strand. At the tip of each strip was a jagged fragment of sheep bone hewn and filed sharp as a razor. After this, what was left of Him carried the beam of His cross as far as He could through the hilly cobblestone streets of Jerusalem, ultimately arriving here at the place of execution just outside the city wall.

Mary was there. So was Beloved John. The Son had expended some of His precious final breaths to address these two directly. To her He had gasped, "Woman, here is your son." And to His best friend, "Here is your mother." (See John 19:26–27.) In His dying moments, with the sin of the entire human race crushing down upon His soul, He paused to arrange for the ongoing care of His widowed mother, who had selflessly and lovingly cared for Him from the moment the angel surprised her with the divine news of His imminent birth until now, the time of His humanly departure from this earth. We can better appreciate how important it was to the Savior to deliver this message if we understand that for a man undergoing Roman crucifixion, each uttered word exacted a terrible price in pain. To breathe, let alone speak, required lifting Himself up on those nail-sundered hands and feet and sliding His mangled back up that splintered beam. Yet He did so, to connect for life these two who had stood with Him to the very end.

Mary Magdalene, out of whom Jesus had cast seven devils, was surely there at Mary's side as well. For six excruciating hours they'd witnessed the slow motion execution-by-torture unfold, their hearts and minds torn with grief and agony as they watched the beloved Savior endure inconceivable and inhuman suffering that seemed as though it would never end. Then, when it was nearly over, two additional figures joined them there at the crest of the skull-shaped outcrop. Two men, both well dressed and clearly influential, stood with John and the two Marys in silent witness of Jesus of Nazareth's final moments of life.

Joseph of Arimathea was both wealthy and a member of the powerful Sanhedrin—the rabbinical court of elders that served as the "supreme court" in religious matters among the Jews of Judea. At some point in Jesus's three-year ministry, Joseph had become a secret believer in and follower of the wonder-working teacher from the north. Alongside him at the cross stood Nicodemus, also a member of the Sanhedrin and a Pharisee. Intrigued by Jesus's power and message, Nicodemus had come to the Rabbi under cover of darkness to learn more. His ears may have been the first to hear Jesus describe the possibility, yes, the absolute necessity, of being "born again."

In those fevered times—with Jerusalem filled with zealots, fanatics, and overheated Messianic expectation—it was dangerous to be associated with a man accused of blasphemy or inciting insurrection. Jesus had been falsely indicted for both. But these men were powerful and well connected. They had little fear of arrest or reprisals from their fellow members of the council or the high priest's guard.

Sadly, the same could not be said for Jesus's closest friends. Save John, they were in hiding. The disciples who had left their nets, their fortunes, their families, their friends, and their futures in order to follow Jesus up and down the coast of Galilee had deserted Him when the authorities and the crowds turned against Him. Peter, their ostensible leader, had boasted of his fierce loyalty. Yet his bravado evaporated like morning mist in the face of a few questions from a servant girl.

Thus those witnessing the death of the loveliest soul to ever grace the soil of this planet, as He made the noblest sacrifice ever undertaken, were pitifully few. The few there who loved Him found themselves far outnumbered by the foul-mouthed executioners, the mockers, and the gawkers.

Huddled together for comfort, they'd looked upon Him as death took its toll. With unfathomable pain and excruciating discomfort, our bleeding Savior had raised Himself one last time and cried out, *"Abba...!"*

This is the Aramaic word that most closely correlates to our English words "Daddy" or "Papa." It is a child's name for a dear and trusted father. Indeed, in many Arabic speaking countries today it remains an infant's first spoken word, just as babies in the English-speaking world babble *"Da-da."*

> [Abba], into Your hands I commit My spirit!
> —Luke 23:46

We'll explore the meaning and implications of that prayer in a later chapter. But for those who were there to hear it launched heavenward, it must have been a startling, jarring moment. Yet no sooner had Jesus's final words echoed back from Jerusalem's stony outer wall than they saw the Master go utterly limp. No more writhing in pain. No more struggling to rise up on nail-riven hands and feet in a desperate quest for breath. No more suffering. Suddenly silence ruled the hill, save the moans of the two criminals to His left and right whose final moments were rapidly approaching.

If Jesus was God incarnate, "the Word made flesh," as John described Him—and He most certainly was and is—then this was the moment God was dead. And if Emmanuel, God with us, had left us, then how could anything ever be good again? How could anything ever be sweet again?

Surely, never again would you press the flushed cheek of a child against yours and feel the vibration of life. Never again would you hear the laughter of children in your home. Never again would you smell the fragrance of a rose. Never again would the flowers bloom. Never again would the joyful sounds of victory be heard. Never again would there be comfort. The death of the Son of God was surely also the death of hope, joy, and peace.

The Father Himself, who carpets the valley in green and nourishes the baby raven, had turned and walked away and left His Son hanging there. Unseen, the demons and the filthy legions of hell's darkened underworld began to clap their fettered hands. In jubilance they hissed at the best heaven had to offer, "He's dead!"

The little group kept vigil there for a few moments more—looking through tear-filled eyes at the pitiful, lifeless figure hanging before them. Some movement to their right caught their attention. They watched as a drunken Roman soldier with a sledgehammer moved to the still-living thief at Jesus's left and, swinging with all his might, shattered the right thighbone of the man. A scream sundered the thick silence and echoed through the Kidron Valley. The man's other leg was crushed in the same way. Then he was quiet. As intended, he could no longer raise himself up on his legs to catch a gasp of precious oxygen. Death came quickly. The soldier then turned to the other thief, and the horrifying process was repeated.

This extraordinary step was not a standard part of Roman crucifixion. It had come at the direct request of the same religious leaders who had lobbied the Roman governor for Jesus's execution. Death by crucifixion could last for days, but these executions were taking place on the "Day of Preparation," that is, the day before the Sabbath. This Sabbath—the eve of Passover. A High Holy Sabbath would commence at sundown. The Jewish authorities convinced the Roman prefect, Pilate, to order the deaths hastened so the bodies could be dealt with before the Sabbath commenced. Also, Mosaic Law required that anyone hanged on a tree had to be buried before sundown so as not to defile the land the Lord had given them, for a hanged man was cursed by God. (See Deuteronomy 21:22–23.)

The group then saw the hammer-wielding soldier turn and walk toward the center cross. Mary cried out in despair and alarm. Joseph stepped forward to have a word with the centurion. "This isn't necessary," he pleaded. "Clearly, this man is already dead." The soldier examined the figure on the cross for a moment and then muttered something in Latin about needing to be certain. So he picked up a spear and rammed it forcefully up and into the side of the battered body, just below the rib cage.

The man on the cross didn't flinch or move in any way at the inflicted wound, but when the spear was withdrawn a cascade of water and blood gushed out in a thick stream. Two millennia later physicians would explain that gradual asphyxiation, such as the one typically endured by a crucified human, results in a rapid and massive accumulation of fluid around the heart. That Roman spear released a flood that testified unequivocally that the Son of Man was dead. But it testified of much more than that.

A lifetime later, when young John had grown bent and frail with age, the only surviving disciple of Jesus and the sole living witness of the events of this day, he would think back to this moment and write:

> There are three that testify on earth: the Spirit, the water, and the blood, and the three are toward the one.
>
> —1 John 5:8

They testify still. And so do those of us who have been washed in that same cleansing flood from the fount that will never run dry! Salvation, healing, deliverance, and an eternal home in heaven are promised to anyone who dares plunge beneath that blessed stream.

The following excerpt from my book *God's End-Time Calendar* is especially insightful on this topic.

> In the record of the teachings of the ancient rabbis, which is called the *Mishnah*, we are told "the Passover wine was said to be red and was to be mixed with warm water."
>
> Ask a rabbi why wine and warm water are mixed, and he will tell you that this mixture of blood and water produces a closer representation of the blood of the Passover Lamb. This ancient tradition begs us to remember that tragic day when the perfect and precious Lamb of God was sacrificed.[3]

Ancient messianic prophecies are fulfilled in these final moments on the cross. "[He] keeps all of his bones; not one of them is broken" (Ps. 34:20), wrote the anointed psalmist in anticipation of the suffering Servant to come. The prophet Zechariah looked down through the halls of future history and caught a glimpse of the Messiah saying, "They shall look upon me whom they have pierced, and they shall mourn for him" (Zech. 12:10, KJV). At this moment, however, the only ones mourning were the pitiful handful huddled together at the nail-pierced feet.

Rough Roman hands quickly removed the bodies of the two thieves and tossed them to the ground as if they were nothing more than the day's trash. The sun was sinking in the reddening western sky. In accordance with common practice of the day, these criminals would be hastily buried in some unmarked mass grave outside the city walls, perhaps near the city's garbage dump. This would be the fate of Jesus as well, except that

Joseph used his power and position to appeal directly to Pilate for permission to claim the body.

Loving hands removed the Master of the wind and waves from the blood-soaked tree and lowered Him gingerly to the ground. His body had suffered enough violence that day as the ugly scourge of sin pummeled the only begotten Son of God. Indeed, in death He was scarcely recognizable even to the mother who gave His body life.

✝ ✝ ✝ ✝ ✝

Time was short. Jesus's body was quickly taken to a place where it could be properly prepared for interment in accordance with Jewish custom. At this point in our narrative we are well served to acquaint ourselves with what those traditions entail.[4] This knowledge will become imperative for understanding the events of the next forty-eight hours.

First, it is vital to understand the importance of burial in Jewish culture. It was considered a catastrophic and shameful thing to not be properly buried. Look, for example, at 1 Samuel 31, where we find King Saul dead from a self-inflicted wound, along with his three sons slain in battle on Mount Gilboa. When the Philistines found the body of the fallen king of Israel, they stripped him of his royal armor and hung his beheaded body from the wall of the Philistine city of Beth Shan.

When word of this reached the Israelites of Jabesh Gilead, they were filled with a holy rage:

> When the inhabitants of Jabesh Gilead heard what the Philistines had done to Saul, all the valiant men arose and went all night, and they took the body of Saul and the bodies of his sons from the wall of Beth Shan, and they came to Jabesh and burned them there. Then they

took their bones and buried them under the tamarisk
tree at Jabesh, and they mourned, fasting seven days.

—1 SAMUEL 31:11–13

Later, those warriors who risked their lives to ensure Saul's
burial received a word of commendation from the new king,
David, who said, "May you be blessed by the LORD, you who have
shown this loyalty to your lord Saul by burying him" (2 Sam.
2:5). Later still, Saul's bones were relocated for burial in the land
of Benjamin, his Israelite tribal home. (See 2 Samuel 21:12–14.)
As we're about to see, it is the bones of a departed person that
matter in this culture, and *where* they rest matters as well.

Only the worst reprobates were destined to go unburied. In
fact, a failure to be buried was viewed as a sign of the judgment of God. Moses once warned the Israelites that if they dis-
obeyed the covenant, they would fall victim to their enemies
and birds and animals would consume their unburied bodies.
(See Deuteronomy 28:25–26.) Centuries later, this very curse fell
upon idolatrous kings Jeroboam and Ahab, along with Ahab's
demonic queen, Jezebel. Concerning these latter two, Elijah's
prophetic warning was grim and grisly: "Dogs will devour
Jezebel by the wall of Jezreel. Dogs will eat those belonging to
Ahab who die in the city, and the birds will feed on those who
die in the country" (1 Kings 21:23–24, NIV).

Clearly the prospect of going unburied was a terrifying one
to the Jewish mind and heart. However, there was a second
reason the burial of the crucified men before sundown was
imperative on this day. The Mosaic Law required it in order to
keep the very land of Israel from becoming defiled:

If a man has committed a sin worthy of death and is executed, and you hang him on a tree, then his body must
not remain all night on the tree, but you must bury him
that day (for he that is hanged is accursed of God) so that

your land may not be defiled, which the LORD your God
is giving you for an inheritance.

—DEUTERONOMY 21:22–23

This explains the Jewish leaders' desire to hasten the deaths
of the crucified men. If the deaths had occurred near or after
sunset, they would have to be left hanging there all through the
Saturday Sabbath, thus violating this scriptural commandment.

By Jesus's day the Jewish practice of burial was well estab-
lished and had two phases, separated in time by a year or longer.
The first phase involved cleaning the body and anointing it with
fragrant oils, waxes, and spices. Then the body (all but the face
and head) was wrapped in strips of linen cloth. After this, more
of the oil and spice mixture was applied to the wrappings. Then
the whole process was repeated. In this way, several layers of
spices and cloths might be applied in total. Finally, a separate
piece of fabric, sometimes referred to as a "napkin," was placed
around the face and head.

The purpose for all of this becomes apparent when you learn
the second phase of the interment process. Once the body had
been wrapped as described, it was customarily placed upon a
shelf or ledge in a small cave. Sometimes a natural cave was
used if available. In most cases, however, a man-made cave was
carved out of the limestone bedrock. These were designed to be
used by entire families and frequently contained several ledges
so more than one body could be accommodated. The tombs of
wealthy or noble families were often situated in a garden, and
frequently the opening of the tomb would be surrounded by a
small courtyard defined by a stone wall.

The prepared body was left there until it completely decom-
posed. This usually required a year or more. Jewish superstition
held that this decomposition of the body served as a form of
atonement for the sins of the person in life.

When only the skeleton remained, a family member would reenter the cave, gather the bones into a bundle, and place them in a stone box called an *ossuary*. The deceased's name and family identification would be carved on the side. The ossuary was then placed in a long-term sepulchre with the bones of other family members. This system allowed for many generations of family members to be buried in a small space. Archaeologists in Israel have discovered hundreds of these ancient sepulchers containing many bone-filled ossuary boxes over the years.

In October of 2002, an announcement electrified the worlds of archaeology, antiquities, and biblical history. An Israeli antiquities collector revealed the existence of a recently recovered ossuary in Jerusalem. The chalkstone box—roughly twenty inches long, twelve inches high, and ten inches deep—dated to roughly the first century AD and contained the bones of an adult male.

What made this ossuary remarkable was the inscription it carried. The following Aramaic words were etched into the side: *Yaakov bar Yoseph akhui d'Yeshua*. Translated into English the box read: "James, son of Joseph, brother of Jesus."

Some were quick to point out that those three names were very common in first century Israel, the equivalent of Robert, William, and Michael in our day. Some authorities in Israel challenged the legitimacy of the inscription, but few questioned the age or authenticity of the box itself. Controversy continues to swirl around the box to this day. Mysteriously, the Antiquities Department of the Israeli government has completely cut off independent researchers' access to the box.

Of course James, the brother of Jesus, was the leader of the fledgling "Jesus Movement" in Jerusalem in the decades after Jesus's ascension into heaven. He became one of the very first early church leaders to be martyred for the faith. Whether this box contains the bones of the biblical James or not, it serves to vividly illustrate the practice of Jewish burial in Jesus's time.

Obviously, this lengthy, multistep process required having access to the tomb and yet finding a way to keep wild animals out. The solution was to place a heavy stone, called a *golel*, in front of the cave opening. It also explains the emphasis on wrapping the body with the oils, spices, waxes, and cloths. Together, these hardened into a type of fragrant shell around the body and kept the stench of decomposition from leaking out of the burial place.

John departed, very likely to find the hiding place of the other disciples and to deliver the news that their worst fears had come to pass. The Master was dead. The Shepherd of the sheep had been struck down. The sheep had scattered.

So, this painstaking process lay before the two Marys, Joseph, and Nicodemus as they took charge of the limp, lifeless husk that had been Jesus of Nazareth. And it had to be done in haste. We don't know precisely where they took Him, but it is reasonable to assume Joseph provided the preparation room. After all, it would be Joseph's recently purchased sepulcher that would soon become the temporary resting place of Jesus's body. Thankfully, the tomb was very close to the place of crucifixion. As John, the eyewitness, reveals, "Now in the place where He was crucified there was a garden, and in the garden was a new tomb" (John 19:41). Thus they did not have to carry the body very far.

Nicodemus was dispatched to quickly acquire the necessary raw materials for the wrapping. As John's Gospel account shows, this was no small task:

> Nicodemus, who at first came to Jesus by night, also came, bringing a mixture of myrrh and aloes, weighing about seventy-five pounds.
> —JOHN 19:39

Seventy-five pounds of precious spices and oils! This must have cost a staggering sum, and it was far more than necessary for the task. Indeed, by some estimates this was enough anointing material to properly bury one hundred common Jewish adults. I use the qualifier "common" because, in accordance with the customs of the day, the more important the individual, the more anointing material would be used in his burial. The Jewish historian Josephus reports that at the death of the revered Jewish rabbi Gamaliel around the year AD 50, roughly forty pounds of anointing products were used in his burial.[5] But here came Nicodemus, staggering under the weight of nearly twice that amount!

Clearly, this secret Jesus follower wasn't preparing for the crude burial of a mere carpenter from the hills of Galilee. He spared no expense, for the honor of helping lay to rest the King of kings had fallen to him.

Meanwhile, the two Marys had been busy in the work of cleaning the blood-covered, wound-riddled body of Jesus. Though they were grief stricken and near the point of physical and emotional exhaustion, they could entrust this work to no other. One last time Mary had charge of the precious Son she carried, birthed, and nurtured. No doubt her weary mind began to race with memories of her Son: His awe-inspiring birth, His teaching in the temple at age twelve, and the extraordinary beginnings of His earthly ministry. There were countless miracles, salvations, healings, and deliverances wrought at His hands, now lifeless, bloodstained, and pulverized with rusty nail marks just below the wrist.

She was determined to properly prepare His body for burial as her work-weathered hands lovingly removed the towel from the washbasin. With care she wiped and scrubbed away the black, caked-on residue that once was His lifeblood. It seemed to coat every square inch of her son's battered body. She began at His head, hoping to somehow find the face she remembered and loved. It eluded her. The damage was too appalling. It was just as the prophet Isaiah had foretold concerning the suffering Servant: "His visage was marred more than any man, and His form more than the sons of men" (Isa. 52:14, NKJV). She would have to rely upon memory.

Was it really thirty-three years ago that she'd brought Him into this world in that Bethlehem barn just down the road, with the horned cattle and bleating sheep to stand guard and only Joseph to serve as midwife while angels sang "Happy Birthday" and shepherds came to see if it was true? Wasn't it just the other day Joseph had placed Him in her still-trembling arms and she'd wiped away the blood and waxy residue of childbirth from His perfect little face? One last time, His face was hers to behold.

She examined a cold, nail-pierced wrist and lifted that gentle hand upward to her lips. She turned it so the palm caressed her cheek, just as it had on those many occasions in life when He calmed her anxious fretting or patiently explained why things were not going to happen the way she'd assumed. Now the hands that had wiped the blindness from Bartimaeus's eyes and performed countless other miracles were lovingly wiped clean of blood.

At His feet, washing and weeping, there was Mary Magdalene. One day, not that long ago, she had anointed these same holy feet with her salty tears and dried them with her hair. Overwhelmed with gratitude for the priceless gift of a purified conscience and a fresh start, she'd taken her dowry— an alabaster box of costly perfumed oil—broken it open, and anointed Him with it. As she worked, she recalled what He'd said that day when His disciples scolded her so. "In pouring this ointment on My body, she did it for My burial," He'd said. "Truly I say to you, wherever this gospel shall be preached in the whole world, what this woman has done will be told in memory of her" (Matt. 26:12–13). That day of burial had now come, and time was not their friend.

Other women were present and helping—significant women. Mark mentions another Mary, the mother of James the Less and Joseph. He also names Salome, the mother of James and John, the wife of Zebedee. It was she who had boldly entreated Jesus to allow her boys to sit at His left and right when He took the throne. Mark explains that these women followed and ministered to Jesus when He was traveling in Galilee. (See Mark 15:40–41.) These too had witnessed the horrific crucifixion, looking on from a distance. John mentions Mary's sister being present at the execution as well (see John 19:25), so it stands to reason that she accompanied her sister to the place where the body of her son now lay.

So with the body washed as well as possible, and Nicodemus having arrived with a staggering quantity of oils and spices, the alternating rhythm of anointing, wrapping, and then anointing again commenced with haste.

Before the job could be completed properly, Nicodemus entered the room. They were out of time. The sun was sinking over the western hills. They could still get the body into Joseph's burial cave before it disappeared completely, but only if they left immediately. The women were dismayed. There was more anointing to be done, and a large quantity of the oils and spices remained unused.

The body of Jesus, wrapped in His winding sheet, was lifted from the table of preparation. The garden awaited.

Chapter 2

INTO the TOMB

"He made his grave with the wicked,"—there was his shame; "but with the rich in his death,"—there was his honour. He was put to death by rough soldiery, but he was laid in his grave by tender women.[1]

> ➤ CHARLES H. SPURGEON
> (1834–1892)

Y OU WILL FIND the Church of the Holy Sepulchre in modern Jerusalem in the Christian Quarter of the Old City at the corner of Ha-Notsrim and St. Helena streets. Many, particularly the world's one-and-a-half billion Roman Catholics and Orthodox Christians, believe the church stands over the site of Jesus's burial place.

The street name "St. Helena" points us to the origin of this belief. Around the year AD 327, Helena, the mother of Byzantine Emperor Constantine, made a pilgrimage to the ruin formerly known as Jerusalem. Constantine converted to Christianity around AD 312 and decreed it to be the official religion of the Roman Empire. I say Helena visited the *ruin* of Jerusalem because the city had essentially been a desolate pile of rubble since being sacked by legions of the Roman general Titus in AD 70. The Jewish historian Josephus described the desolation in these terms:

> Jerusalem...was so thoroughly razed to the ground by those that demolished it to its foundations, that nothing was left that could ever persuade visitors that it had once been a place of habitation.[2]

Sixty-five years later, the Roman Emperor Hadrian destroyed what little had been rebuilt while putting down the final Jewish rebellion in the Second Jewish War of AD 135. After this second devastation, Hadrian renamed the city "Aelia Capitolina" and built several temples to the Roman gods on the ruins of the city, including a temple in the northwest quarter of the city dedicated to the worship of Venus (the Roman corollary to the Greek's Aphrodite).

Roughly two hundred years later, Helena made her trip to Jerusalem in search of holy relics related to her new Christian faith. One of her first stops happened to be the site of Hadrian's temple to Venus. Her son had ordered the pagan temple demolished and a church erected in its place.

Orthodox tradition states that while at the demolition site, she came across some timber fragments near a tomb hidden underneath the temple. And since humans possess a remarkable ability to find what they're looking for and see what they're hoping to see, she returned home declaring she'd found the remnants of the "true cross" of Christ and the tomb where He had been buried. What is more, she found them essentially in the first place she looked!

The basilica erected by Constantine in the place of that pagan temple was burned by Muslim invaders in AD 614 and destroyed by Muslim conquerors in AD 1009. The basilica that stands today was built in phases over the centuries since. Today it attracts hundreds of thousands of pilgrim visitors each year who line up to catch a glimpse of the tomb of Jesus's burial and resurrection. But there have always been serious questions about whether this was truly the area of the Old City in which Jesus had been crucified and buried. Many doubt that the pilgrims are looking at the correct tomb.

For one thing, fierce debates among archaeologists have raged for centuries as to where the ancient city walls of Jerusalem actually ran at the time of Jesus's execution. It is a given that the site of the Crucifixion, and therefore also of the burial, was just outside the walls of the city. But because of the repeated destructions and rebuildings of the city through the centuries at the hands of Romans, Byzantines, various Muslim caliphates, and European crusaders, determining where those walls originally stood is no easy thing to do.

In 1867 another leading candidate for the site of Jesus's interment arose. Just beyond the Damascus gate on the Old City's northern side, a German theologian and amateur archaeologist discovered a rocky knoll known to some of the local shepherds and Bedouins as "skull hill." Many local traditions identified the area as an ancient "necropolis," or cemetery, and also a place of execution, particularly stoning. Further exploration of the area in the late 1800s revealed numerous tombs along with an ancient wine press and a cistern, suggesting the area had once been a garden. Since that time, the most impressive of these tombs has come to be referred to as "the Garden Tomb." It has become for the world's Protestant pilgrims to Jerusalem what the Church of the Holy Sepulchre is for the world's Catholics and Orthodox—that is, the definitive burial place of Jesus. Tour buses by the thousands stop here each year and disgorge armies of believers toting cameras and taking "selfies" with their smartphones. Yet, like the other traditional site, there are legitimate doubts as to whether this is indeed the tomb in which the body of Jesus was laid on that Friday evening.

Thus, the actual location of the Crucifixion and Resurrection remain the subject of debate. Perhaps this is for the best. Maybe our hunger for a *place* to venerate and focus our awe upon is misplaced.

Jesus told the Samaritan woman at the well that a day was coming in which neither Mount Zion in Jerusalem nor Mount Gerizim in Samaria would be the focal point for true worship of God. He shocked her religious sensibilities and upended her paradigm by describing a coming day in which geography would become utterly irrelevant to those who would serve and honor God:

> Jesus said to her, "Woman, believe Me, the hour is coming when neither on this mountain nor in Jerusalem will you worship the Father...Yet the hour is coming, and is now here, when the true worshippers will worship the Father in spirit and truth. For the Father seeks such to worship Him. God is Spirit, and those who worship Him must worship Him in spirit and truth."
> —JOHN 4:21, 23–24

Yes, more than sixteen centuries ago, a half-pagan Byzantine queen mother went searching for relics in hopes that they carried supernatural power to heal or protect. But this is not what Jesus died and conquered Death itself to endow to this world. The blood-bought, born-again believer possesses the *same* Spirit that raised Christ from the dead with ample power to heal, protect, and deliver! (See Romans 8:11.) We have no need of holy sites. Everywhere the foot of a child of God treads is holy ground.

We have no need to seek out the spot where Jesus was buried, for the Risen One dwells in our very hearts. Even if the burial place of Jesus could be identified beyond all doubt or debate, we would find no life-transforming power in it. For since the Day of Pentecost, the Power that empties tombs resides in us through the mighty baptism in the Holy Spirit.

✝ ✝ ✝ ✝ ✝

The setting sun slowly brought the curtain down on both the Passover and "Day of Preparation" for the Sabbath—Nisan 14 by the Hebrew calendar. The Sabbath commenced at sundown, initiating the weeklong Feast of Unleavened Bread, making this new day doubly holy and therefore doubly restrictive in terms of permissible activity. In other words, there was more to do and less time in which to accomplish it. As a result, everyone was seemingly in a hurry on this day. This included those who wanted to see Jesus of Nazareth dead. As John explains, these were compelled to expedite their grisly work:

> Since it was the Day of Preparation, to prevent bodies from remaining on the cross on the Sabbath day (for that Sabbath day was a high day), the Jews asked Pilate that their legs might be broken, and that they might be taken away.
>
> —JOHN 19:31

Afterward, it was the grieving caretakers of Jesus's body who were forced to make haste. As two noble and respected members of the Jewish Sanhedrin rushed to arrange for the burial of Jesus's shattered body, another type of preparation was taking place in a nearby barley field on the edge of Jerusalem.

The barley and wheat fields all over the Land of Promise were planted in the fall and harvested in spring, the barley ripening first. It was harvest time in Israel, but the Law of Moses forbade anyone from partaking of the harvest until the high priest had offered the firstfruits.

Thus in this chosen field, temple priests took consecrated ceremonial scythes and cut down some of the standing grain stalks. They bundled the stalks and tied them with cords into a "sheaf" of barley. They then clearly marked the sheaf with a ribbon and left it in a corner of the field where it would remain for two days—that is, until after the next day's Sabbath.

All of this was done in accordance with the ancient tradition handed down by God to Moses for the upcoming Sheaf Offering. This ancient harvest ceremony—part of the Feast of Firstfruits—would take place in the temple courtyard on Sunday. On that day the grain from that designated "first" sheaf of the harvest would be ground into flour and placed in a bowl. Then the high priest would lift this bowl, or *omer*, heavenward and invoke God's blessing upon it and, by extension, all of the harvest that followed.

The Feast of Firstfruits and its centerpiece, the Sheaf Offering, carried significance in another key respect. It was the day that marked the fifty-day countdown to *Shavuot*, the Feast of Pentecost or Weeks, wherein they not only celebrated the end of the harvest season but also commemorated when Moses gave the Torah to the children of Israel in the desert. Without the Sheaf Offering there could be no Pentecost. Of course, there could be no Sheaf Offering without a sheaf.

Thus, on Friday evening the high priest Caiaphas was obligated by duty to oversee this setting aside of the ceremonial sheaf. He was exhausted but euphoric. He had been up all of the previous night seeing to the arrest, trial, and execution of that rabble-rouser from Galilee. Much to his relief, this was finally done and he was forever rid of that threat to peace and stability. After all, as long as the Romans were in control of the land, any threat to peace and stability was a threat to his power, prestige, wealth, and comfort. There would be some time to rest on tomorrow's Sabbath Passover. Then he would be back in the public eye once more on Sunday for the Firstfruits ceremony of the Sheaf Offering. He had no idea the role he had played in the fulfillment of this ancient ritual.

The Apostle Paul would one day describe Jesus in His resurrection as the "first fruits" of all who have died. (See 1 Corinthians 15:20.) But before the grain could be lifted up on Sunday, it had to be cut down on Friday. This had been the day of cutting down. The day of lifting up was two sunrises away.

† † † † †

Seven centuries before the extraordinary events of that evening, the prophet Isaiah was granted a momentary flash of special sight or foreknowledge. The Spirit of God folded the fabric of space-time in order to give the prophet a glimpse of where God's scarlet thread of redemption would one day lead, that is, to Calvary's blood-soaked hill. He saw a man despised and forsaken by His friends. He saw "a man of sorrows and acquainted with grief" (Isa. 53:3). He saw a man wounded and bruised for the transgressions of a fallen humanity. He saw a man covered in "stripes" that carried the power to heal the diseases unleashed upon the world in Adam's fall. He saw the crushing weight of the sin-guilt of all mankind laid upon this man by God Himself.

Then he saw this man in death, and what he saw made no sense. It was a seeming contradiction. A paradox:

> For he was cut off out of the land of the living; for the transgression of my people he was struck. *His grave was assigned with the wicked, yet with the rich in his death.*
>
> —Isaiah 53:8–9,
> emphasis added

"How can this be?" the prophet surely wondered. How was it possible that a man could be assigned to be buried with wicked men and yet be with rich men after His death? A burial with the malefactors seems plausible for a man who has had His soul stained with the uncleanness of every sinner who has ever lived or ever will live. Yes, this fits the prophet's cultural paradigm. But then to see Him in the company of elite society at His death? To see Him embraced and honored by the noble in His passing? There was no way to make sense of this. Yet he wrote what he saw.

More than seven hundred years later, men gently carried the hastily wrapped and anointed body of the Son of David through the nearby garden and into the waiting tomb. Perhaps Joseph and Nicodemus carried Him personally. If not, Joseph's servants were given the task. In any event, Jesus had been assigned a burial in a shallow, unmarked pit alongside thieves and murderers and rapists. Yet here He was, with two wealthy noblemen in His death. Isaiah saw what he saw. The prophecy was sure and accurate.

We know in hindsight what the prophet did not. Once sin's penalty had been paid, there was no longer any need for the Son of Man to continue to be "despised and rejected of men." The great preacher of old, Charles Spurgeon, took note of this shift in an 1894 sermon delivered in the famed Metropolitan Tabernacle in London. He keenly observed:

> Now, rich men must come and do Him homage and, accordingly, Joseph and Nicodemus came. It may seem only a little thing, but it indicates the turn of the tide, just as the floating of a straw may do. Jesus is no longer derided, nor even attended only by the poorest and most obscure of Galileans, but Joseph from Arimathea, and Nicodemus, a ruler of the Jews, attend the funeral of the

great Lord and Savior of men—and so pay such honor as
they can to His dead body![3]

Mary and the other women waited in the small outer court of
the sepulchre. It would be unseemly in this culture for women
to be in such close proximity to the men in public. Besides, the
tomb itself was a very confined space.

When John wrote of this moment many decades later, he
took pains to point out that this was a freshly carved tomb,
and added the detail, "in which no one had ever been buried"
(John 19:41). Our previous examination of Jewish burial customs makes clear why John mentions this. He made sure future
skeptics and doubters would know that no other bodies were
already undergoing decomposition in this space, nor were there
any ossuary boxes filled with bones stacked inside. It was a
thoroughly *empty* tomb into which Jesus's body was laid.

So, one of the niches within the hand-carved cave was
selected, and the linen-wrapped body was carefully laid to rest
there. Now the final step, the wrapping of the head with the
linen napkin, could commence.

Perhaps His mother entered to perform this task. The others
drew back to provide her some private space in this moment.
The sun had set now and the light was rapidly waning. It was
dark within the tomb, so she completed her work as much by
touch as by sight. She was loath to leave, hoping to prolong this
final, tender good-bye. Yet she was compelled by pleas from
outside to abandon her eldest son to the cold, dark tomb. She
exited and every present male was recruited to assist in rolling
the *golel*, the great stone, into place. Then a second smaller
stone, called the *dopheq* was wedged in place at the base of the
larger one, much like wooden blocks are sometimes used by
mechanics to "chock" the wheels of vehicles today. The purpose

of this smaller stone was to keep the larger stone from shifting or rolling out of place.

Mary Magdalene was deeply distressed that the wrapping was done hastily and the anointing was incomplete. It wasn't right. He deserved better, she protested through tears.

Joseph reassured her that she and the other women might return the morning following the Sabbath to do a more thorough job of anointing the body. Perhaps he agreed to meet her there so she could gain access to the tomb. But for the moment they had to get off the streets. The Sabbath was commencing. Nicodemus's fellow Pharisees were policing the city for Sabbath violators.

The group led the shattered mother of Jesus away, half-carrying her. Presumably, she was escorted to the residence of John, who would see to her care from that day forward, just as her eldest son had requested in His dying moments.

Even so, two of the women could not bring themselves to leave Him alone there. As Matthew revealed, "[Joseph] rolled a large stone to the door of the tomb and departed. Mary Magdalene and the other Mary were there, sitting opposite the tomb" (Matt. 27:60–61). This "other Mary" was probably "Mary the wife of Clopas" mentioned by John as having been with Jesus's mother at the cross.

Heartbroken, bewildered, and exhausted, these two devoted Jesus followers collapsed on a stone bench opposite the now-sealed sepulchre under the gathering twilight. We are not privy to their words or thoughts, but again, Spurgeon's inspired insights illuminate our understanding of this detail in the Bible narrative:

> They had seen where and how the body was laid, and so had done their utmost, but yet they sat watching still: love has never done enough, it is hungry to render service.

They could scarcely take their eyes away from the spot which held their most precious treasure, nor leave till they were compelled to do so the sacred relics of their Best Beloved.[4]

These women of Galilee had been there from the very beginning. They most likely were present at Jesus's earliest days of ministry, witnessing His first miracle at the wedding in Cana, and a little later in that same city the healing of the gravely ill son of a royal official with just a word from His lips. They would have heard the excited chatter that swept across Capernaum and throughout all of the northern territory after Jesus healed a demoniac in the middle of the synagogue. These two handmaidens to the Prince of Heaven had not only witnessed an incredible array of miracles by His hands, but also at least one of them was a living example of His power to deliver.

The Bible does not reveal the time, nor place, nor any other detail of Mary Magdalene's life-transforming encounter with Jesus. Luke merely mentioned, almost in passing, that she was a woman "from whom seven demons had come out" (Luke 8:2). Surely years of incessant torment and oppression made her a reviled, lonely outcast. A lifetime of bondage to a snarling pack of foul, defiling spirits would have twisted this pitiful woman's mind and soul into a picture of pain. Then she met a man with unfathomable compassion and incomprehensible spiritual authority. One stern command from His grace-filled mouth shattered her fetters and freed her spirit. For the first time in memory she was whole. At peace. Clean.

What deep reservoirs of gratitude must have resided in the heart of such a woman! No wonder she could not stop staring at that ponderous stone barrier that held her Savior captive.

No wonder she and her companion sat in stunned bewilderment at the events of those twenty-four hours. Nothing made sense. How could things have turned out that way? All they knew was that they loved Him. They believed in Him. Yet there He was—broken, cold, and lifeless in that limestone prison.

It is natural at this point to wonder where the rest of Jesus's inner circle was throughout the earth-shaking events of that day. As we've seen, the women were all bravely present and active at every horrifying turn in that grueling march. But where were the men?

We find our answer in the back half of Matthew 26:56. A simple eight-word indictment written by one of the indicted:

Then all the disciples forsook Him and fled.

Matthew knew. He was there with Jesus and the other ten on the Mount of Olives. He was among those who couldn't manage to honor the anguished Savior's pleas to remain awake with Him and pray. He was present when Judas joined them in the Garden of Gethsemane and embraced the Master, marking with a kiss the correct target for the high priest's armed guards hiding in the shadows. He'd seen Peter's impulsive, panicked lunge at one of the guards that severed the man's right ear, followed by one last act of healing mercy by the Great Physician, who simply touched the ear and restored it completely.

Matthew had felt fear wash over the entire group like a great wave as those guards bound Jesus and roughly shoved Him down the hill, punching and kicking Him as they went. He had participated in the chaotic, panic-fueled chatter that immediately followed. "We've got to get off this hill," someone had shouted over the din. "The next group of guards will be coming for us!" He had added his agreement to the consensus that they should break up into smaller groups and find safe places to hunker down in the city. Yes, Matthew knew. They all had forsaken Him. They all had fled.

Of course, Jesus had foreseen this. So had the prophet Zechariah. Mark records how only hours before Jesus's arrest He had warned them, "All of you will fall away on account of Me this night" (Mark 14:27). Then He had quoted the prophet: "For it is written: 'I will strike the shepherd, and the sheep will be scattered.'" (See Zechariah 13:7.)

Scatter they did. Only Peter had dared linger for a while longer on the shadowy perimeter of the crowd waiting for the Sanhedrin's show trial to commence at Caiaphas's palatial residence. Yet the instant he had been recognized as a member of Jesus's inner circle, he too had fled to the shelter of a bolted door amid Jerusalem's teeming Passover masses.

When the striking of the Shepherd began in earnest, the sheep scattered.

✝ ✝ ✝ ✝ ✝

At last, the light of day surrendered. By Hebrew reckoning it was a new day, Nisan 15, the Sabbath. For roughly fifteen hundred years, Israel's most faithful honored the Sabbath day and kept it holy, as God directed through Moses. This was the fourth of God's Ten Commandments etched on tablets of stone by His own finger. In issuing this ordinance, God explicitly tied the observance of the Sabbath to His activity at Creation, explaining, "For in six days the LORD made heaven and earth, the sea, and all that is in them, and rested on the seventh day. Therefore the LORD blessed the Sabbath day and made it holy" (Exod. 20:11).

Setting all labor aside every seventh day served as a powerful reminder that God is the Author of creation. He knows the Sabbath is important to your spirit, soul, and body. Mark 2:27 tells us "the Sabbath was made for man, and not man for the Sabbath." It's meant to follow God's pattern of creation and be observed one day out of every seven on which we rest from our labors and focus on God. Let me remind you, the Sabbath is not your obligatory Sunday morning hour-long church service! Psalm 23:2 plainly states, "He *makes* me lie down." How blessed are we to serve a gracious, loving Father who desires that we cease from our labors and rest to refresh every part of our triune being.

For six days God worked, declaring each phase of His work "good" as He moved on to the next. After six days of creative activity, the world was perfect and whole. Then the earth's designated steward, Adam, allowed it to become twisted and distorted by disobeying the one stipulation set before him in that beautiful garden paradise—not to eat of the tree of the knowledge of good and evil.

The unspoken message of the Sabbath is a reminder of a past day in which man didn't have to sweat and grovel in the dirt to scrape and scratch out a living. Yet it also points to a future day, one in which that curse will be rolled back.

Now in the hills of Judea a new Sabbath had begun. For six days in Jerusalem Jesus carried out the work of redemption, fulfilling prophecy at every turn. That work culminated in the grueling sixth day, now completed. The heroic and herculean work of redeeming mankind was done. The Author of redemption had ceased from His labors.

Indeed, just before He expired, He declared, "It is finished." Now came the day of rest.

PART II:

SATURDAY

Chapter 3

INTO HIDING

*How could it have entered the mind of any writer
to venture the prophecy that a Jew who had been
crucified, whose whole life had seemingly been
proved by that cross to be an utter failure and
whose disciples had utterly forsaken Him in the
end—that He would conquer the world by them?*[1]

> ANDREW MURRAY
> (1828–1917)

SILENCE RULED THE garden and its lonely hillside tomb.
Stillness presided within and around the sepulchre that
cradled the linen-wrapped body of the precious Lamb
of God. The Sabbath sun had climbed Judea's green eastern
hills and cast long shadows across the stirring city. For Jerusalem's many Romans, Greeks, and Hellenized Jews—a sizable
minority of the population in these cosmopolitan times—this
was just another day. Business would be transacted. Chores carried out. Meals cooked. Burdens carried.

Not so for most of the city's inhabitants. For the tens of thousands of pious Jews who still called Jerusalem home, along with

the hundreds of thousands among the far-flung Diaspora who had "gone up" to Zion to observe the Feast of Unleavened Bread, this was a sacred day of rest. This day's meals were arranged in advance the day before, resulting in the common identifier, "the Day of Preparation." Today, no work was permitted until the sun set once more.

Even so, amid the many secularized Jews and pagan foreigners on the street this early morning, we cannot help but notice a cluster of men dressed in the unmistakable and ostentatious manner of the Pharisees hurrying down the dusty street. They could not be more conspicuous. In their midst we note a man wearing the ornate robes and prominent headpiece of the high priest.

Having departed his personal palace in the Upper City, a wealthy section inhabited by the city's upper crust, Joseph Caiaphas, accompanied by his phalanx of Pharisees, lesser priests, and Sanhedrin sycophants, was making his way toward the nearby Praetorium within Herod's magnificent palace complex on the Temple Mount. He had requested and received another audience with the Roman prefect, Pontius Pilate, who resided in the Praetorium when in Jerusalem.

Pilate visited Jerusalem only when he must, and he must during the great pilgrimage feasts such as Passover. It was those times—when the city's population swelled from roughly forty thousand souls to more than two hundred fifty thousand religious zealots—that trouble was most likely to break out. For most of the year Pilate lived in a fortified governor's residence in the coastal city of Caesarea, seventy miles to the north. He much preferred the cool Mediterranean breezes to the stifling heat, dust, and animal stench of overcrowded Jerusalem.

It had scarcely been twenty-four hours since Caiaphas and his entourage were at Pilate's doorstep prodding him to condemn to death the Galilean wonder-worker. Although reluctant at first, Pilate had ultimately agreed to their demands. Yet here they were at his doorstep once more, and with another request.

Among the writers of the four New Testament Gospels, only Matthew, the former tax collector with long-standing relationships and connections to Roman government officials, brings us details of the conversation that transpired on that Sabbath Saturday morning. He writes:

> The next day, following the Day of Preparation, the chief priests and Pharisees gathered before Pilate, saying, "Sir, we remember that deceiver saying while He was still alive, 'After three days I will rise.' Therefore command that the tomb be made secure until the third day, lest His disciples come by night and steal Him away, and tell the people, 'He has risen from the dead.' The last deception will be worse than the first."
>
> —MATTHEW 27:62–64

Weary and ever cautious, Pilate assented to their request. With a dismissive wave of his hand he told them, "You have a guard. Go your way. Make it as secure as you can" (Matt. 27:65). To a Roman military man, the term "a guard" carried a very specific meaning. A guard is four soldiers. The group departed with the quartet of armed, uniformed Roman combat veterans who constituted the first watch. The Sanhedrin members of the entourage likely knew precisely where the Galilean was buried, because Joseph of Arimathea was a fellow member of their council. Some would certainly be privy to the whereabouts of their colleague's recently commissioned sepulchre.

Within the hour, a melted wax seal bearing the insignia of the Roman government was affixed to the stone that barricaded the entrance to Jesus's tomb. This seal was most likely placed at the seam where the *dopheq*, or small "chock block" stone, was wedged against the *golel*, the larger stone. In this way, any disturbance or movement of the stones at all would be revealed by cracks in the hardened wax. After the seal was in place, the guards were left behind with strict orders to let no one near the tomb.

Future generations of theologians and Bible expositors would debate whether these guards were Roman soldiers or members of the high priest's "temple guard." The preponderance of evidence suggests it was the former.

First, if only Jewish temple guards were to be stationed at the tomb, Caiaphas would have no need to seek the Roman prefect's help in obtaining them. The temple's security force was at his command. He could have simply ordered it so, and it would have been done.

Second, Matthew used several Greek words to refer to the guards, specifically *custodies*, from which we get our English word "custody," and *tarountes*, which translates to "the watch." Most significantly, Matthew also called them *stratiotas*, which simply and straightforwardly means "soldiers." (See Matthew 27:65.) Matthew used this same term in 27:27 to refer to Herod's Roman troops who dragged Jesus to the Praetorium and, with the rest of the Roman cohort, mocked and beat Him.

No, these were trained, highly disciplined fighting men of Rome stationed in this garden. These men knew well that the penalty for falling asleep on watch was death. They settled in, and for the next several hours, the boasts, laments, profanities, and idle chatter of homesick soldiers defiled the stillness of the garden where the body of the blessed Son of God had been laid.

Meanwhile, somewhere amid Jerusalem's densely packed guest houses and sleeping quarters, several clusters of men sat out the Sabbath in the icy grip of fear, grief, and confusion. In three years of following Jesus, they had gradually come to believe that in Him the glory of Israel was about to be restored. They surely thought they would be high-ranking officials in this restored Davidic regime. Now the disciples' dreams of glory for their nation and themselves lay dashed to pieces in tiny shards around their feet. Their movement was seemingly outlawed. The turncoat Judas was rumored to be a suicide.

Their initial terror at the prospect of being arrested, tortured, and executed, just as their leader had been, had not dissipated after a sleepless night. Indeed, a number of them would most likely have already slipped out of town if it weren't for the Sabbath's restrictions on travel. Only the shortest of journeys were permitted on that day.

The ban on Sabbath travel was rooted in the ancient Israelites' experience in the wilderness, where God miraculously provided a two-day supply of manna on the sixth day so they could obey God's command to remain at home on the seventh. In Exodus 16:29, God decreed, "Every man remain in his place. Let no man go out of his place on the seventh day." Naturally, over the centuries the interpreters of the Jewish law found loopholes and exceptions to this "stay at home" mandate. Initially, travel within the city was allowed on the Sabbath, but never beyond. Then the lawyers found a way to sanction travel of two thousand cubits beyond the walls of the city, but not a cubit further.[2] Eventually the upper limit was doubled to four thousand cubits and then doubled again to eight thousand.

This distance became known as a "Sabbath walk" or a "Sabbath day's journey." Note the use of this term in Acts 1:12: "Then they returned to Jerusalem from the Mount of Olives, which is a Sabbath day's walk from Jerusalem." This indicates that the distance from the Mount of Olives back to the nearest city gate was just within the limit for Sabbath travel.

As a result, escape from the city on Saturday was not an option for the disciples. They would have been too conspicuous on the mostly-empty roads and byways if either the high priest's spies or the Roman authorities were looking for them.

However, at first light on Sunday, two unnamed disciples would slip through the city gates and head for the town of Emmaus, seizing their very first opportunity to escape the perceived danger of Jerusalem. We will encounter these two and their journey a little later.

Today, however, the surviving eleven of Jesus's inner circle simply lay low while trying to process the inconceivable events of the previous week. Only last Sunday Jesus had been the hero of Jerusalem's adoring throngs. In the little village of Bethany just outside the city, a town still vibrating with the electrifying news of His raising His friend Lazarus from the dead, He had mounted a donkey colt and ridden toward Jerusalem.

His disciples followed along, reveling in the joy of being identified with Him. They had come to believe that He was God's "Christ"—the Anointed One foretold by the prophets and eagerly anticipated by every devout Israelite of that generation. Yet up until that point, Jesus had resolutely insisted on keeping His power and authority a well-guarded secret. Time and again He had performed some exceptional miracle of healing or deliverance and then exhorted the blessed and jubilant recipient not to tell anyone that it was He who had made it possible. His modesty and stealth had been so very frustrating to them. Now, at last, He was allowing Himself to be revealed and exalted. Surely now the kingdom was to be restored to Israel. Best of all, they were the handpicked regents of the soon-to-be King! "And what better time than Passover for Him to be revealed?" they must have thought as Jerusalem's magnificent Herodian architecture crowned by the gleaming golden temple came into view. After all, it was on the evening of the very first Passover that God had struck down the firstborn of the Egyptians and thereby set the stage for the Israelites' deliverance from bondage. Now, roughly fifteen hundred Passovers later, it seemed a Moses-like deliverer was about to remove the Roman foot from Israel's neck.

All along this journey of less than two miles, the crowds had hailed this loving teacher and wonder-worker as Israel's promised Deliverer. The closer they got to the Holy City, the more exuberant the ovation had become. Soon the masses were singing a hymn of praise reserved for the promised Messiah of Israel: "Hosanna! 'Blessed is He who comes in the name of the Lord!' Blessed is the kingdom of our father David that is coming in the name of the Lord! Hosanna in the highest!" (Mark 11:9–10). Palm branches and even cloaks and tunics were thrown into the road to blanket Jesus's pathway to the citadel from which His glorious ancestor, David, once ruled. Oh, what a heady day that had been.

The disciples' sense of expectancy only grew when, a day later, He'd shocked His followers and enflamed the temple establishment by turning the temple's court of the Gentiles upside down, figuratively and almost literally. Filled with a holy anger they'd never before witnessed, their leader and friend went on a rampage, upending merchant stalls and kicking over carts. This startling outburst only served to further fuel their belief that something big—something extraordinary—was about to happen.

Meanwhile, the miracles and wonders just kept coming. They'd heard Him speak a curse over a leafy green but fruitless fig tree one day and noticed that it was completely dead the next. They'd heard Him pray and then heard God reply with a thundering voice from heaven. (See John 12:28.)

What is more, some of the things He'd said in recent days comported perfectly with their belief that a visible, tangible Israelite kingdom was about to emerge, with their close friend taking His place as king on David's restored throne. For example, immediately after they'd all heard that audible voice from heaven, Jesus had declared:

> Now judgment is upon this world. Now the ruler of this
> world will be cast out.
>
> —JOHN 12:31

"Now...Now!" He'd said that word twice! Surely the coming judgment He spoke of was the judgment of their Roman oppressors. After all, the only "ruler of this world" they knew anything about was the Roman Emperor Tiberius. Yet, at the same time, other things He'd said during the week made no sense at all in the light of these glorious expectations, particularly His bewildering and cryptic comments about the temple being torn down, with not one stone being left upon another.

Now, in the space of less than eight days, the disciples of Jesus had plummeted from the heights of ecstatic euphoria to the depths of disillusioned despair. Their leader was dead and buried, their movement outlawed, and the fickle tide of public opinion had turned against them. Indeed, it all now seemed like a three-year-long fever dream. Now each man would need to decide where he would go from here. In the disciples' minds, the glory road they believed they were traveling suddenly appeared to be an utter dead end. Their obvious skepticism in the face of the first reports of Jesus's resurrection made it clear they considered Him gone forever.

In reading and rereading the Gospels, as we have the privilege of doing today, it is easy to wonder why Jesus's disciples were so shocked by His death and so painfully slow to believe He had risen. After all, over the course of the year preceding the events in Jerusalem, Jesus had repeatedly mentioned both His death and His conquest of it. To be certain, some of His references were somewhat veiled and arcane. On more than one occasion He had declared that this generation that constantly clamored for "a sign" would get none from Him other than "the sign of Jonah." In retrospect, with minds illuminated by the Holy Spirit, the disciples realized this was a reference to Jonah having spent three days in the dark belly of a great fish before being returned to light and fresh air of a Ninevite beach. Nonetheless, the closer Jesus got to the climax of God's redemptive plan, the more plainly He spoke about what was coming.

For example, in the sixteenth chapter of Matthew we find the account in which Jesus asked His disciples, "Who do you say that I am?" In response, Peter had his Holy Spirit-enabled epiphany, "You are the Christ, the Son of the living God" (Matt. 16:15–16). After plainly admitting that He was indeed the Messiah, He, true to pattern, forbade them from telling anyone. Then suddenly the One who so often spoke in parables and cryptic metaphors became jarringly literal and frank:

> From that time on, Jesus began to show His disciples that He must go to Jerusalem and suffer many things from the elders and chief priests and scribes, and be killed, and be raised on the third day.
> —MATTHEW 16:21
> (SEE ALSO MARK 8:31–33; LUKE 9:22)

All three of the Synoptic Gospels record this shift toward plainspokenness concerning what was about to transpire. Jesus laid out the sequence of events so simply even a child could comprehend it. In the statement above, Jesus declared He would:

1. Go to Jerusalem.

2. Suffer many things.

3. Be killed.

4. Be raised on the third day.

Not only did Jesus state this plainly on this occasion, the Word of God declares that Jesus kept giving them this information "from that time on." It is also apparent that Peter understood the message Jesus was delivering. Matthew records that Peter rebuked the Son of God. "This shall not happen to You," he said.

A chapter later in Matthew, Jesus again tells them plainly, "The Son of Man is about to be betrayed into the hands of men, and they will kill Him, and He will be raised on the third day" (Matt. 17:22–23). Again, His message seemed to be understood because Matthew records that upon hearing this, the disciples "were extremely sorrowful." Not long afterward, He told them yet again:

> Now we are going up to Jerusalem, and the Son of Man will be betrayed to the chief priests and scribes. And they will condemn Him to death and deliver Him to the Gentiles to mock, and to scourge, and to crucify Him, but on the third day He will rise.
> —MATTHEW 20:18–19

Again we see the four critical elements of what will transpire—Jerusalem, suffering, death, and rising. So how is it possible that these men could be so utterly taken by surprise and thrown into despair when these very events unfolded? How could the possibility of Jesus rising from the dead not even enter the minds of those who had seen Him break up no fewer than two funerals by raising up the deceased—one of whom had been dead more than three days?

In fact, in that day following the Crucifixion, Jesus's enemies seemed far more aware of His past predictions than did His friends. For example, Jesus had made His "sign of Jonah" statement to the temple scribes and Pharisees. (See Matthew 12:38–40.) The symbolism was not lost on them. Memory of this statement prompted their early morning trip back to Pilate and drove their urgent request for a guard on the tomb. Their precise words were:

> Sir, we remember that deceiver saying while He was still alive, "After three days I will rise." Therefore command that the tomb be made secure until the third day, lest His disciples come by night and steal Him away, and tell the people, "He has risen from the dead." The last deception will be worse than the first.
>
> —MATTHEW 27:63–64

The enemies of Jesus remembered His promise. Why didn't His friends? It is a mystery. Still, we must not be too hard on them. We too are frequently guilty of faulty memory or faltering faith concerning promises our Lord has made to us. There exists a very common, very deeply innate tendency for all of us to take special note of what fits our preconceptions and gloss over things that don't. We hear what we hope to hear. See what we hope to see. We love evidence that validates our preferred way of thinking about things, and we easily dismiss evidence to the contrary as being irrelevant or flawed.

In our day, behavioral scientists have a fancy word for these very human tendencies. They call them *cognitive biases*. Back where my roots run deep in the hills of eastern Kentucky, we called them "knot-heads!" In our postmodern era, we hear endless talk about paradigms and preferred narratives. The fact is, we all have the capacity to ignore what's plainly before our faces if we prefer something different to be true. Denial can, in fact, be a powerful blinder.

In any event, it seems that every mention the Savior made to His followers regarding His impending sacrifice was rationalized away as a metaphor or symbolic language or something that simply wasn't true because it *could not* be true. It was only after the drama had fully played out and the illuminating force of the Holy Spirit, the One who brings "all things to their remembrance," had taken up residence in their minds that His words sank in. Only then would the lights finally come on. "Of course!" they would one day exclaim. "He told us all of that must take place. It was God's plan all along. Why couldn't we see it?"

In fifty days, immediately after being filled with the Holy Ghost on the Day of Pentecost, timid Peter would jump up and boldly preach the very first Spirit-led sermon. In this extemporaneous message delivered to a Jerusalem festival throng, he would declare that Jesus's arrest was "by the ordained counsel and foreknowledge of God" (Acts 2:23). He would show them from the Scriptures how the psalmist David foresaw his Messianic descendent being put in a grave and yet not suffering corruption (vv. 27–31).

Yes, in a few weeks it would all be very clear, and the disciples would recall that He had told them plainly and repeatedly all these things would happen. But here on the Sabbath of despair, there was no room for light or hope in the minds of Peter and the others. Fear, confusion, and disappointment filled every available space in their souls.

At some point Saturday evening, a message stealthily made its way to the disciples' various Jerusalem safe houses. The shattered eleven reassembled as a group late that night for the first time since fleeing the Mount of Olives in a panic two nights previously. It is very likely their chosen meeting place was the same Upper Room in which they'd eaten that final meal together.

Walking back into that room was a wrenching experience for each of them, but for Simon Peter most of all. Here, forty-eight hours earlier, the beloved Creator of the universe had stooped to wash *his* feet like a household slave. Peter, staring at the spot where Jesus had reclined as they ate, remembered how He'd said one of their group was about to betray Him. The bombshell statement sent a shockwave of speculation and self-examination through the group at the time. Now they knew. It was Judas, the one now absent from their ranks. He was now lying dead and unburied in a garbage pit ravine.

Peter probed his grief-fogged memory, struggling to recall other things the Master had spoken that night. What was it He'd said as He snapped the crisp unleavened bread into smaller portions? Oh yes! "This is My body." Then He had taken the wine cup and said something about His blood and a "new covenant." It made no sense at the time, and Peter could make no sense of it now. He could not help jumping with alarm every time he heard a hand upon the door latch.

Once all had arrived, the group huddled together and instinctively looked to Peter, James, and John for leadership. Their three faces looked just as bewildered and frightened as those of the other eight. There were no answers there.

† † † † †

We have looked in on this Sabbath Saturday and observed the activity of the high priest, the Sanhedrin, and the Pharisees. We have watched the movements of the frightened disciples. We have even taken note of the tedious work of the Roman guards in that silent cemetery.

Yet a key question remains unasked. Where was Jesus? What, if anything had He done on this day?

Certainly, we know of Jesus's activity on Friday. His work was visible for heaven, earth, and hell to witness at the top of Calvary's hill, on a cross where the furious love of God intersected with the broken and shattered hearts of humanity. Never before and never since has love been on open display as it was that day, strung up between heaven and earth with the piti-less Palestinian sun beating down on His bare wounds until it felt as though the very flames of hell had embedded themselves in the flesh of the only begotten Son of God. Yes, He busied Himself suffering and dying for the sins of the world—for your sins and mine.

Likewise, every saint with a Bible can tell you what Jesus would be doing the next day, on Sunday. Numerous witnesses saw His movements and reported His words. There are no mysteries surrounding Friday or Sunday.

Not so of Saturday. Yes, we know His body was lying quietly in the garden sepulchre with Roman guards biding their time just beyond the massive stone barricade at its entrance. But it is not the disposition of Jesus's *body* that is at issue here. Where was His *spirit*? Was there additional redemptive work to accomplish in the unseen realm? Precisely how did Jesus spend this Sabbath? In heaven? In hell?

It is time to probe the deepest of mysteries. We must now turn to the infallible Word of God to search out the inscrutable truth.

Chapter 4

INTO the HEART of the EARTH

I believe in Jesus Christ . . . who was conceived by the Holy Spirit, born of the Virgin Mary, suffered under Pontius Pilate, was crucified, died, and was buried. He descended into hell . . .

> THE APOSTLES' CREED

A GROUP OF ABOUT fifty stands in what used to be the "mosh pit" of a downtown nightclub in a major city of the United States. On the small stage, where heavy metal rock bands once performed, another sort of band prepares to play. The crowd is young and diverse, many adorned with tattoos and piercings. There are women with hair in every color of the rainbow. Among the leather and denim–clad participants are a few young white-collar professionals and hipsters.

Suddenly a man wearing a T-shirt and tattered jeans appears on stage. The band begins to play a contemporary worship song, a slide projector flickers to life, and the group begins to recite the words on the screen before them: "I believe in God the Father Almighty, Maker of heaven and earth. And in Jesus

Christ, His only Son, our Lord, who was conceived by the Holy Spirit…"

This is the Apostles' Creed. Like the Nicene Creed and the Athanasian Creed, believers in Jesus Christ have recited it for centuries. It was created to remind the faithful of the fundamental doctrines of the faith and to draw a bright, clear line around the boundaries of Christian orthodoxy. In the ancient world, when the vast majority of converts to faith in Jesus Christ were illiterate and had no access to a Bible in their own language, the creeds of the church—recited weekly from memory—served a vital purpose. They acted both as guide to doctrinal truth and as protection from doctrinal error.

Then in the sixteenth century came the earthquake of the Protestant Reformation, animated by both the advent of the printing press and the translation of the Scriptures into the respective tongues of the common man. As a result of this spiritual revolution, the creeds diminished in importance. Indeed, they were never again prominent within the evangelical branch of the Protestant family tree. Now, though, they are enjoying a remarkable resurgence among young Christians who are weary of both postmodern relativism and therapeutic pop preaching. In these ancient words this new generation of believers are discovering what the earliest Jesus followers cherished: a sense of being rooted in something larger and grander than themselves. In an age of isolation and superficial "social media" relationships, these public declarations of the Apostles' Creed offer connection to a community of common belief and to the teachings of the risen Christ.

For the benefit of the unfamiliar, here in its entirety is the more traditional version of the Apostles' Creed as it has been recited in various languages from as long ago as the fifth century:

> I believe in God the Father Almighty, Maker of heaven
> and earth. And in Jesus Christ his only Son our Lord;
> who was conceived by the Holy Ghost, born of the Virgin
> Mary, suffered under Pontius Pilate, was crucified, dead,
> and buried; he descended into hell; the third day he rose
> again from the dead; he ascended into heaven, and sitteth
> on the right hand of God the Father Almighty; from
> thence he shall come to judge the quick and the dead. I
> believe in the Holy Ghost; the holy catholic[1] Church; the
> communion of saints; the forgiveness of sins; the resur-
> rection of the body; and the life everlasting. Amen.

The doctrines defined in this timeworn edict are almost uni-
versally accepted across the myriad expressions and forms of
Christianity around the world—with one key exception. One
phrase in this and the other traditional creeds of the church
has tended to generate discord throughout history. It still does
today.

In the original Latin, the phrase in question is *descendit
ad inferna*. In English, this is, "He descended into hell," just as
the ancient creeds render it.

Did Jesus's spirit indeed plummet into the dark, cavernous
underworld of the region of the doomed and the damned souls
in hell while He was in the tomb? If He did not, why has this
assertion plainly been a part of the confession of believers since
the time of the earliest church fathers? And if Jesus's spirit did
descend into the domain of hell while He was in the tomb,
other questions present themselves. What did Jesus experience
there? Did He suffer there as a sinner? Or did He vanquish His
archenemy and the very adversary of the soul of mankind as
reigning King and Conqueror?

Because of the uncertainty and disagreement surrounding
questions such as these, the clause, "He descended into hell,"
remains by far the most controversial in the great creeds of the

church. Indeed, some denominations consider it optional or refuse to include it at all.

Most of the Reformers wrestled with the issue, often in the context of addressing the Roman Catholic doctrine of purgatory. For example, John Calvin, in his epic *Institutes of the Christian Religion*, addressed the question at length, ultimately citing his agreement with Thomas Aquinas that Jesus had indeed descended into hell prior to His resurrection.[2] In 1533 in Torgau, Germany, Martin Luther, standing in the pulpit of the very first Protestant church ever built on German soil, delivered a message in which he plainly stated that Christ descended into hell.[3] These and many other messages and declarations on the subject through the centuries were necessary precisely because there were, and are, such varying views about where Jesus's spirit was in the hours between the time of His death on the cross and His resurrection.

Even the magnificent evangelist Charles Spurgeon wrestled with the question and ultimately expressed uncertainty. On a crisp October Sunday morning in 1869, in a message entitled, "Christ with the Keys of Death and Hell," Spurgeon said:

> Whether when our Lord died, His soul actually descended into hell itself, we will not assert or deny—elder theologians all assert that He did, and therefore they inserted in the Creed, the sentence, "He descended into hell," meaning, to many of them, at any rate, hell itself. It was not till Puritan times that that doctrine began to be generally questioned when it was, as I think rightly asserted, that Jesus Christ went into the world of separated spirits, but not into the region of the damned. Well, it is not for us to speak where Scripture is silent, but why may it not be true that the great Conqueror cast the shadow of His presence over the dens of His enemies as He passed in triumph by the gates of hell?[4]

In the 1990s, one prominent Christian college skipped over the phrase entirely in a series of chapel messages about the Apostles' Creed because not one of the institution's twelve professors of Bible or theology believed it to be true.[5]

Does it really matter? After all, the disposition of Jesus's spirit in those deathly hours has never been a central element in the gospel message. I have seen no one on any side of the issue make the argument that where one stands on the question affects a person's salvation or standing with God. In other words, there is no litmus test for orthodoxy here.

In contrast, the Bible is clear and emphatic about how Jesus was and is both wholly God and fully man. The Word of God unapologetically states that belief in Jesus coming in the flesh, living a sinless life, dying for mankind's sin and rising on the third day is essential for saving faith. The full-throated affirmation of these propositions is the very mark of a Christian. One cannot doubt these things and expect a place at the table of the community of believers who truly trust in God.

It is not the same on the question of where Jesus was or what He did while His body lay in repose in that limestone tomb in that rocky hillside garden. The Bible is too mysterious on this matter for it to be made a test of fidelity. A few intriguing scriptures offer hints and suggestions, but they do not make firm declarations.

Thus reasonable people may and do disagree about the exact sequence of events that occurred after Jesus yielded His spirit on the cross and His body was laid in the tomb of Joseph of Arimathea. We should, however, be able to agree on this point. He—that is, Jesus's spirit, not His body—was *somewhere* during the time between His death and His resurrection. Nothing in Scripture suggests that any person's eternal spirit sleeps or goes dormant.

So, let us search the Scriptures with a keen spirit and an

open mind to examine the evidence, seek understanding, and perhaps in the finding, gain a deeper appreciation for the magnificence of our Champion.

"He descended into hell." Before we can evaluate the truth of that claim we must, of necessity, define terms. What, or where, is meant by *hell*?

You and I tend to read that word with a post-Calvary mindset. Most of us learned early in childhood that after death a person immediately finds himself or herself either in heaven or hell. Even those who grew up in non-Christian homes have this understanding. Of course, most individuals' concepts of both destinations are shaped more by popular culture and movies than by Scripture. Sadly, most movies on the subject of heaven and hell too often miss the mark of true spiritual reality because they're produced by those in the secular arena who don't recognize or possess accurate biblical knowledge or even have a slight foundation of the Word of God. Instead, they opt for "supernatural" content to mesmerize the viewers and warrant top sales at the box office. Therefore, far too many people carry around in their minds a Hollywood heaven and a cartoon hell.

The point is, we tend to assume that instantaneous heaven or hell after death has always been the fate of individuals after dying. Yet the Bible suggests this wasn't always the case. In other words, we must begin by recognizing that the disposition of the dead *before* Jesus conquered Death might have been different than *after* He conquered it.

Numerous Old Testament scriptures make reference to *Sheol*, the collective abode of all the dead, both righteous and wicked. In the ancient narrative of Job, the man of suffering asks, "Will they go down to the gates of Sheol? Will we descend together in the dust?" (Job 17:16). Repeatedly the psalmists reference *Sheol* as the gathering place of the dead, as when David declared, "The cords of Sheol surrounded me; the snares of death confronted me" (Ps. 18:5).

The Jewish understanding in Jesus's time was that *Sheol* was divided into two domains. The first was called Paradise or Abraham's Bosom, and was the gathering place for God-fearing and righteous souls. The second was a place of torment for the unrighteous dead.

Adding to the confusion, Jesus also made several references to *Hades*. In Greek mythology, *Hades* was the god of the underworld, the ruler of the realm of dead souls. In Jesus's day, Greek culture had so infused the vocabulary of the times, the word *Hades* had come to be used interchangeably with the Hebrew term *Sheol*. The two were synonymous, which is why most of our English Bibles translate both *Sheol* and *Hades* as "hell."

An illuminating parable of Jesus presupposes and features these two separate but linked locales within the realm of the dead. In the sixteenth chapter of Luke, Jesus illustrates a point by describing two individuals, an unrighteous wealthy man and a righteous beggar. As the Savior describes it:

> It came to pass that the beggar died and was carried by the angels to Abraham's presence. The rich man also died and was buried. In Hades, being in torment, he lifted up his eyes and saw Abraham from a distance and Lazarus in his presence. So he cried out, "Father Abraham, have mercy on me, and send Lazarus to dip the tip of his finger in water and cool my tongue. For I am tormented in this flame."
>
> —LUKE 16:22–24

Here in red letters—in Jesus's own words—we have the two separate domains of *Sheol* or *Hades* described. In this parable, it is revealed that although these two realms are visible to one another, a "great gulf" or chasm separates them, making travel between the two impossible. (See Luke 16:26.)

One of these is clearly a very unpleasant place to be. Additional scriptures in the New Testament also reinforce this idea that *Sheol/Hades* is a temporary place where souls are kept as they await the final resurrection and judgment at God's throne.

In addition to this, Jesus also spoke of a place called *Gehenna*—a Greek adaptation of a Hebrew name for the valley of Hinnom, which had become a garbage dump for the city of Jerusalem. The fires that burned there continuously made it an appropriate example for the term *hell*—a place of unquenchable fire. It seems clear that Jesus had Gehenna in mind when He spoke of the fiery penalty of the unrighteous dead. Furthermore, Revelation 20:11–15—the passage that describes the Great White Throne Judgment—indicates a clear distinction between *Hades*, a temporary place of torment, and the "lake of fire," a future permanent one. When people today, including many Christians, hear the term *hell* they immediately think of the lake of fire. Is it any wonder they recoil at the suggestion that Jesus descended there?

So let us be clear. When it is suggested that Jesus "descended into hell," the implication is that Jesus entered the realm of the dead—a realm that, at that time, contained both Abraham's Bosom (or Paradise) for the righteous dead and a prison involving unrelenting torment for the unrighteous dead. With this foundation we can now begin to explore this question in the reliable light of Scripture:

Precisely where was Jesus's spirit in the interim between His death and resurrection?

† † † † †

There are a number of intriguing scriptures that suggest Jesus had vital, unseen work to do in those silent hours. These verses persuade me that on this Saturday, while the disciples hid and the earthly high priest prepared to carry out his duties concerning the Feast of Firstfruits, Jesus—our everlasting High Priest—was actively accomplishing some necessary tasks as well. In other words, even in death, Jesus still asked, as He once did as a boy, "Did you not know that I must be about My Father's business?" (Luke 2:49).

One of the most interesting statements Jesus made concerning His death and resurrection appears in the twelfth chapter of Matthew. There He says, "For as Jonah was three days and three nights in the belly of the great fish, so will the Son of Man be three days and three nights in the heart of the earth" (v. 40).

We will address the issue of reconciling Jesus's "three days and three nights" statement with His actual time in the tomb in a later chapter. What I want to point out now is that Jesus used the Greek word *kardia* here in the phrase translated "in the heart of the earth." This is obviously the root of our English word *cardiac* and can indeed refer to the physical blood-pumping muscle in the chest cavity. However, this word was also used figuratively by Greek speakers of Jesus's day to describe the center or core of a thing, just as we use *heart* figuratively in the phrase "heart of America" and when my home state is described as "Ohio, the heart of it all."

When Jesus said He would spend three days in the *kardia* of the earth, He equated it with the way Jonah spent three days in the belly of a great fish. This would seem to imply more than simply entering a tomb carved into a rocky hillside. The heart of the earth suggests something deeper. Could that something deeper be *Sheol*?

For additional light, let us examine a key Messianic prophecy in the Old Testament. In Psalm 16:10, the forerunner priest-king David writes from the vantage point of his promised descendant, the future Priest-King who would one day crush the serpent's head. David foresees a death, but with a twist at the end:

> For You will not leave my soul in Sheol, nor will You suffer Your godly one to see corruption.

There are two things to note concerning this remarkable glimpse of the future Messiah's thoughts and His faith in God's faithfulness. First of all we see that His "soul" will indeed enter "Sheol," but will not be left there. This is an unambiguous prophetic decree that the promised Messiah will die and then be resurrected. This is one of many Old Testament prophecies that made no sense to the Hebrew mind prior to the advent of the Holy Spirit, but afterward shouted of fulfillment in Christ. The second half of the verse concerns not the soul of the Messiah but rather His body. The Messiah is affirming His trust that God will not allow His physical body to undergo "corruption," that is, decay.

It's illuminating to note that in the Jewish way of thinking about death, decay of the body commenced on the fourth day after death. This belief is evident in Martha's warning to Jesus at the tomb of her brother Lazarus: "Lord, by this time there is a stench, for he has been dead four days" (John 11:39). In the light of David's prophecy, one wouldn't have necessarily needed to hear Jesus's frequent references to being raised on "the third day" in order to know the day of rising. If the Father was not going to allow His beloved to suffer corruption as the psalmist prophesied, then He would have to rise on or before the third day.

Not only did David give an accurate prediction of the Messiah's bodily resurrection, he also declared His soul would not remain in *Sheol*, which can mean either the grave or the place of the departed dead.

So which did David foresee? Did he glimpse the future Messiah simply resting in the grave, or did he literally see His spirit descending into the realm of dead souls? Peter actually answers that question for us. In the same spontaneous sermon I cited previously—the one that stands as the first Holy Spirit-anointed and inspired sermon ever delivered by a person other than Jesus—Peter quotes this psalm of David, citing it as proof that Jesus was resurrected from the dead. In quoting it, however, Peter used the Greek word *Hades* rather than the word for "grave."

> Brothers, I may speak confidently to you concerning the patriarch David, that he both died and was buried, and his tomb is with us to this day. But being a prophet, and knowing that God had sworn with an oath to him, that of his seed according to the flesh, He would raise up the Christ to sit on his throne, he foresaw this and spoke concerning the resurrection of the Christ, that His soul was not abandoned to Hades, nor did His flesh see corruption.
>
> —ACTS 2:29–31

Jesus offered another clue to this mystery while He was yet on the cross. When the repentant thief on His right cried out, "Lord, remember me when you come into your kingdom," Jesus responded by promising the dying man something much more wonderful than merely being remembered:

Jesus said to him, "Truly, I tell you, today you will be with
Me in Paradise."

—Luke 23:43

You will recall that "Paradise" was one of the two sections
of *Sheol*, the destination of the righteous dead prior to Christ's
resurrection. It was a place of comfort, but was temporary,
where those who died in faith awaited the fulfillment of the
promise to be present with the Lord in heaven. Jesus replied
to the penitent thief's request for remembrance with an even
better promise. The thief refers to some vague future date. The
dying Last Adam says, "today!" It seems reasonable to deduce
that Jesus is saying that before the sun sets on this momentous
Friday, they shall both be standing in the realm of the righteous
dead. Spurgeon had this reality in mind when he once called
the penitent thief both "our Lord's last companion on earth"
and His "companion at the gate of paradise."[6]

This, of course, prompts yet another question. *What did the
Son of God do there?*

The Apostle Paul's God-given revelation concerning the
person and work of Christ is of immense value in answering
this question. For example, in Ephesians 4:8–10, Paul, speaking
of Jesus's death, resurrection, and ascension to heaven, says:

> Therefore He says: "When He ascended on high, He led
> captivity captive, and gave gifts to men." (In saying, "He
> ascended," what does it mean but that He also descended
> first into the lower parts of the earth? He who descended
> is also He who ascended far above all the heavens that He
> might fill all things.)

This passage has perplexed many throughout history. Some
view Paul's mention of *descending* and *ascending* as merely
referring to the fact that the Son of God came down from

heaven to live on earth as a man, and then ultimately returned up to heaven. It is true that our Lord did these things, but there is clearly far more implied here than that.

Paul is referencing Psalm 68:18. This psalm of David is a war song in which God is portrayed as a victorious Warrior-King who possesses thousands upon thousands of chariots and, in the eighteenth verse, leads "captivity captive." This passage pictures the victorious King as receiving spoils from the enemy and passing them along to His subjects as gifts:

> The chariots of God are twice ten thousand, even thousands of thousands; the Lord is among them, as in Sinai, in the holy place. You have ascended on high, You have led captivity captive; You have received gifts from people, yes, even from the rebellious, that the LORD God might dwell among them.
> —PSALM 68:17–18

These two related passages prompt some questions. What enemy was spoiled? What was his domain? Who were the captives led captive? And who are the "men" with whom the conquering King shares the spoils of conquest in the form of "gifts?" Let us engage Paul as our interpreter. In other words, let us allow Scripture to interpret Scripture. Paul tells the Ephesians that the psalmist's phrase "He ascended" implies that the conqueror must have "descended first into the lower parts of the earth."

Now Paul's phrase, "lower parts of the earth," could simply be referring to Jesus's burial in a cave, but this seems unlikely, especially in the light of several other intriguing New Testament passages. Look, for example at these extraordinary words of Peter:

> For Christ also has once suffered for sins, the just for
> the unjust, so that He might bring us to God, being
> put to death in the flesh, but made alive by the Spirit,
> by whom He also went and preached to the spirits in
> prison, who in times past were disobedient, when God
> waited patiently in the days of Noah while the ark was
> being prepared, in which a few, that is, eight souls, were
> saved through water.
>
> —1 PETER 3:18–20

Here we have another passage that has puzzled many and
vexed more than a few. Peter, in the context of encouraging
believers who were suffering persecution for righteousness'
sake, points to Jesus's suffering and "death in the flesh." Then,
in what reads like an aside or a digression, he mentions that
Jesus "went and preached to the spirits in prison," taking special note of those who existed prior to Noah's flood. Some have
speculated that these confined spirits are actually demonic
spirits that were active on the earth in that undeniably wicked
period. Others assume that the prisoners are the spirits of the
wicked dead.

The passage raises many questions, but what seems clear is
that Jesus indeed made an appearance in *Sheol* following His
death. Peter plainly says Jesus preached to the imprisoned spirits
there. The Greek word translated "preached" in this passage is
kerusso, which in other places refers to an announcement by a
herald or messenger. In other words, what Jesus delivered to
these imprisoned spirits wasn't so much a sermon as we usually
think of such, but rather a proclamation. Peter doesn't reveal
the details of this announcement, but we can assume it has to
do with the titanic shift in spiritual power and authority on the
earth that had just been wrought by Jesus's work on the cross.
Satan had fallen into the trap. A transfer of the ownership of an
important set of keys was taking place. Those in the realm of

Death would be the first to hear about it because they would be the first to be affected by it.

Let us add to this evidence a remarkable statement by the Apostle Paul along these same lines. In Colossians 2:15, the great evangelist says concerning Jesus, "And having disarmed authorities and powers, He made a show of them openly, triumphing over them by the cross."

Paul's language here evokes the Roman Triumph—the lavish victory parades through the streets of Rome staged by the Senate to celebrate great military successes. This was imagery every reader in Paul's day would instantly recognize and understand. Whenever a Roman general conquered a new land, his triumphal return to the capital city would take the form of a procession showcasing his spoils of war to Rome's cheering throngs. This parade usually included the shackled, vanquished enemy king in a humiliating spectacle of subjugation. This is the image Paul invokes in explaining to the believers in Colossae what Jesus accomplished through His sacrifice and ensuing victory over Death. In His death and resurrection, Jesus Christ made a public display of all the forces of darkness, manifesting His absolute mastery over them in a spectacular demonstration of His overwhelming authority and victory. This is why Jesus could rightly say immediately before His ascension into heaven, "All authority has been given to Me in heaven and on earth" (Matt. 28:18).

Combine these scattered pieces of biblical evidence and a remarkable narrative begins to emerge. Do you recall Jesus's final words upon the cross? Luke notes them for us:

> And Jesus cried out with a loud voice, "Father, into Your hands I commit My spirit." Having said this, He gave up the spirit.
>
> —LUKE 23:46

As Luke the meticulous physician and historian makes clear, Jesus's spirit left His body the instant He died. So let's deduce where His glorious, perfect spirit went, in the light of the truths we have just examined. According to the picture we have assembled, His spirit descended into Paradise, or Abraham's Bosom, the righteous side of *Sheol* within the domain of Death. While there, Jesus made some type of proclamation or announcement to the imprisoned spirits in that place.

He would soon lead the righteous souls in Abraham's Bosom into the presence of the Father at His resurrection. Those unrighteous souls in *Hades* would be left behind, remaining there in torment until the time of the final judgment. (We'll discuss this in more detail in a later chapter.)

I am convinced this is a reasonable explanation of the various biblical statements, hints, and clues we've examined. Even so, it is an interpretation only.

Did Jesus's spirit visit *Sheol* while His body lay in repose in the garden tomb? I am confident in saying, "yes." Did His soul suffer torment there, as some assert? That is a completely different question. Let us examine it together.

Over the years a number of well-meaning Bible teachers have contended that Jesus's atoning work wasn't completed on the cross, but rather continued in the uttermost regions of hell right up until the moment of the Resurrection. They reason that since Jesus paid the penalty for our sins, and that penalty included suffering in hell, Jesus therefore must have endured the torment of hell as part of His redemptive work. They point to some of the scriptures we have examined—the ones indicating Jesus "descended" into Sheol at death—to bolster this claim.

I believe those who proclaim this have seriously misunderstood the Bible's teaching concerning the redemption Jesus wrought on our behalf. Allow me to offer three biblical reasons Jesus did not need to descend into hell to finish His atoning labors.

First, there are the words of our Savior from the cross. You will recall Jesus's statement to the penitent thief, "Truly, I tell you, today you will be with Me in Paradise" (Luke 23:43). The Greek word translated "today" in Jesus's declaration is unambiguous in meaning. It means *today*. This is a dying man making a solemn promise to another dying man. "This very day you and I shall stand together in Abraham's Bosom, the place of peace and reward for the righteous dead within Sheol."

Then there is Jesus's cry, "It is finished!" uttered shortly before expiring. In my previous work *The Cross: One Man...One Tree...One Friday...* I plumbed the rich depths of meaning hidden within that simple three-word sentence:

> When John, the beloved disciple, recalls this statement to record it in his Gospel narrative, he uses a Greek accounting term—*tetelestai*. Future English translations of John's Gospel will render that term in a way that tends to strip it of the legal and financial connotations. They translate it, "It is finished" (three words for one). But *tetelestai* does not mean merely that a thing has ended. It has a far greater implication than merely a clock has run out and the game has concluded. It is a declaration that all has been accomplished. All that was lacking has now been supplied. The breach has been healed. The debt has been fully satisfied. Shalom—nothing broken, nothing missing.[7]

Nothing broken. Nothing missing. Nothing. Jesus covered it all—salvation, healing (of spirit, soul, and body), and deliverance, all through the shedding of His blood and His death upon that cruel, rugged beam. All sickness, disease, affliction, and addiction was atoned for, the price paid in full by our loving Savior, as was forgiveness of our sins.

Isaiah 53:4–5 reminds us, "Surely he has borne our grief and carried our sorrows; yet we esteemed him stricken, smitten of God, and afflicted. But he was wounded for our transgressions, he was bruised for our iniquities; the chastisement of our peace was upon him, and by his stripes we *are* healed" (emphasis added). The reiteration of this scripture in 1 Peter 2:24 reminds us that we *were* healed. If you *are* healed and you *were* healed, you must *be* healed!

I recently walked through one of the most sobering experiences of my life as I faced the greatest challenge to my physical health that I have ever encountered. I was diagnosed with cancer of the right vocal cord. Me—Pastor Rod Parsley—attacked in the very instrument that God had used as a mighty force for His kingdom for the past forty years. I have devoted my entire life to preaching the good news of the gospel and ministering the healing and delivering power of the Lord Jesus Christ to hundreds of thousands of people through the years and witnessed countless miracles as a result!

As I struggled to comprehend the extent of this assault and believed God for the manifestation of the healing that Jesus provided for me on Calvary, the revelation of the finished work of Christ became more real to me than the radiation treatments I was undergoing at the time. My faith in the area of divine healing and health was reignited as I pondered and meditated on healing scripture after scripture on a daily basis. God ministered to me and reminded me over and over that my healing was provided for every bit as much as the forgiveness of my sins by my suffering, bleeding Savior on Calvary's hill. In Malachi 4:2 we're reminded that "the sun of righteousness will rise with healing in its wings." I am assured He would not have risen from the grave unless my healing was a finished work! So today I thank Him for total and complete healing in my body—nothing broken, nothing missing!

Christ's emphatic proclamation from the cross assures us that *every* necessary aspect of the redemptive act was accomplished and nothing further needs to be done.

Second, in addition to Jesus's *words* from the cross, we must examine what the Bible says concerning the *work* of the cross. Put another way, what does the New Testament declare "the gospel of Jesus Christ" to be?

The cross stands as the centerpiece of Paul's preaching. "We preach Christ crucified," he bluntly explained to the believers in Corinth (1 Cor. 1:23). To the Colossians Paul declared that through Jesus's work God reconciled all things in heaven and on earth to Himself "through the blood of His cross" (Col. 1:20). Over and over Paul defined the gospel in terms of Jesus's work on the cross—and only the cross:

> He blotted out the handwriting of ordinances that was against us and contrary to us, and He took it out of the way, *nailing it to the cross*. And having disarmed authorities and powers, He made a show of them openly, triumphing over them *by the cross*.
>
> —Colossians 2:14–15,
> EMPHASIS ADDED

Paul never once hinted that anything in addition to the cross was necessary to make atonement for sin. The work at the cross was a complete and accomplished fact.

Third, we must take particular notice of what the Scriptures say concerning the *washing* of the blood. Over and over, the infallible Word of God lifts up the blood and the blood alone as the necessary agent of redemption. For example, Jesus Himself told His disciples at their final meal before His death that the wine represented "My blood of the new covenant, which is shed for many for the remission of sins" (Matt. 26:28).

Come with me on a whirlwind tour down the New Testament's crimson highway. Let us stop at Romans 5:9 to learn that we are justified by His blood. Follow me now to Ephesians 1:7, which stands to testify that we are redeemed by His blood. A stop at Hebrews 10:19 reveals that we have access to the Most Holy Place through Jesus's blood. Then at 1 Peter 1:19 we learn that we have not been redeemed with perishable things like silver or gold, but "with the precious blood of Christ."

Run with me now to the twelfth chapter of Revelation, to the very throne room of heaven, where we see Satan, the old accuser of the brethren cast down, defeated, and humiliated by victorious saints whose sins have been cleansed by the precious blood of the Lamb. How can this be? "A loud voice in heaven" has our answer (v. 10). "They overcame him by the blood of the Lamb and by the word of their testimony, and they loved not their lives unto the death" (v. 11).

It is the shed blood of Jesus Christ that effected our glorious redemption. Thus, with the saints of old we can joyously sing, "There is a fountain filled with blood drawn from Emmanuel's veins; and sinners plunged beneath that flood lose all their guilty stains!"[8]

The witness of Scripture is absolute and undisputable. The cross where Jesus shed His utterly innocent blood is sufficient for the redemption of mankind. When Christ gave His life upon the cross, He did all that needed to be done.

This means that His trip to the realm of the dead was a journey of unparalleled victory rather than one of continued suffering. He arrived in Paradise a victor bringing good news for the righteous souls gathered there, and a sobering announcement for the spirits imprisoned on the other side of the "great gulf." (See Luke 16:26.)

His work was complete. All that remained was to await the appointed moment of reemergence from that dark, dank tomb. The fulfillment of the "sign of Jonah" requires more time in the heart of the beast.

Meanwhile, heaven, earth, and hell waited in silent expectation. Breathlessly the angels kept watch over the rocky hillside garden, staring transfixed at that massive sealing stone, straining to detect the slightest hint of movement. The pervading question permeating all of creation still remained, "Will Father God veto the crucifixion of His only begotten Son with a resurrection?"

Chapter 5

GRAVEYARD PLANET

He who burst the bars of death was thereby declared to be the Son of God with power. Since the resurrection morning there has never been—there could not be—the slightest question as to His final rulership of the world. Death was conquered, Satan was conquered, and He proclaimed the wearer of the name above every name.[1]

> E. P. GOODWIN
> (1832–1901)

THE RESURRECTION OF Jesus of Nazareth was by no means the first instance recorded in Scripture of someone being raised again to life from the icy tentacles of death. Nor was it the last. When Jesus spoke of dying and then living again, His Hebrew hearers could have called upon their knowledge of the Old Testament's rich history and cited numerous accounts of miraculous resurrections.

There was the widow of Zarephath's only son in 1 Kings chapter seventeen. Three times the prophet Elijah stretched himself out over the body of that deceased boy in earnest prayer. On the third effort, the power of God radiated through him and restored the young man to his jubilant mother.

In similar fashion, 2 Kings chapter four records how Elisha returned to a Shunammite woman her miraculously resurrected child, long after he had passed over into Sheol. In chapter thirteen of that same chronicle of Israel's history, we find that so much power remained on the one who had requested and received a double portion of Elijah's anointing that even Elisha's dry bones carried the tangible, transferable power of the anointing to restore the dead to life!

Yes, when Jesus, speaking metaphorically of His own body, looked the haughty Jewish leaders in the eye and said, "Destroy this temple and in three days I will raise it up," His disciples should have had some inkling as to what He meant. After all, on three separate occasions they had witnessed with their own eyes the dead obeying the command of Jesus.

They were with Him that day in Nain when they had encountered a funeral procession. A widow woman robbed of her only son, and with him any hope of being sheltered and cared for in her fragile older years, walked beside the wooden box carrying his remains. "Do not weep," He had instructed her. The confusion on her grief-wracked face melted into joy unspeakable and full of glory when, at His next words, her son sat straight up in that coffin and began to speak. (See Luke 7:11–15.)

They were there in Capernaum in Galilee when He arrived seemingly too late to rescue Jairus's precious twelve-year-old daughter from the grip of death. They should have known that "too late" is a meaningless term when the Author of time and space is speaking. "Little girl, arise," He had said. Suddenly, a gasp of breath broke the ensuing silence. Blue lips flushed warm and pink. Eyelids fluttered. Shouts of unbridled, delirious euphoria filled a house that only moments before had been filled with the anguished wailing of mourners. (See Luke 8:40–56.)

They had also been there outside of Bethany when Martha met Him with news of His dear friend Lazarus's death. Once again "too late," as the heartbroken sisters had reminded Him. There at the rock-hewn tomb they had seen the Master weep in empathetic identification with His beloved friends' grief. Yet only a moment later He commanded the stone be removed from the sepulchre of a man four days dead.

One shouted command later, that "dead man" staggered out of his dark tomb and into the brilliant golden light of the Judean sun as he struggled to free himself of his winding sheet. (See John 11:17–44.)

They were there. They had seen these wonders. They beheld His glory. And yet when it happened, it still took them utterly by surprise.

The important thing to note about all of these previous resurrections is that they had been only temporary reprieves from the certainty of eventual death. Each of these reanimated demonstrations of God's power succumbed some time later to the disease our forefather Adam passed on to us all. As the writer of Hebrews once emphasized, every man or woman ever born has an appointment to keep: "It is appointed unto men once to die" (Heb. 9:27, KJV).

Yet His own resurrection, which Jesus both hinted at and declared openly, was of a different character than these. He had made this plain to grieving Martha on that Bethany roadside. She had spoken of her hope in a certain future resurrection of the righteous that would include her brother. Jesus had both validated and focused her hope with His response:

> I am the resurrection and the life. He who believes in Me, though he may die, yet shall he live. And whoever lives and believes in Me shall never die.
>
> —JOHN 11:25–26

Then He followed His earth-shaking declaration with a simple but vitally important question. He asked her, "Do you believe this?"

I must ask you the same question: do you believe this?

He'd called it "the sign of Jonah." A pious delegation of scribes and Pharisees approached Jesus one afternoon. They arrived with great pomp and ceremony. They were on a mission. They insisted on seeing His divine credentials. "Teacher, show us a sign," they demanded. Jesus showed little interest in revealing Himself to skeptics and hypocrites:

> But He answered them, "An evil and adulterous generation seeks after a sign, and no sign will be given to it except the sign of the prophet Jonah. For as Jonah was three days and three nights in the belly of the great fish, so will the Son of Man be three days and three nights in the heart of the earth."
>
> —MATTHEW 12:39–40

On two other occasions in Scripture, Jesus mentioned this "sign," but in those instances did not mention "three days and three nights." Even so, both Bible-believing laypersons and theologians alike have grappled over the years with the task of reconciling Jesus's "Jonah" analogy with the timeline presented in the Gospels. In other words, if Jesus was crucified on Friday, buried at sunset on Friday evening, and rose from the grave sometime early Sunday morning, how can He be said to have fulfilled His own "sign of Jonah" prophecy? After all, by our modern, Western methods of counting days and time, Jesus spent at most two nights and one day in the belly of that hillside tomb.

Some have attempted to resolve this apparent discrepancy by suggesting that Jesus was not crucified on a Friday at all, but rather on Wednesday. They believe the integrity of God's Word is at stake. So with the best of intentions, they go to great lengths to try to harmonize the biblical narrative's mention of milestone markers as the Passover celebration, the pre-Sabbath "day of preparation," and the Sabbath itself, with a Wednesday crucifixion.

There is an assumption driving these noble efforts. Many assume that Jesus's reference to "three days and three nights" requires the passage of three literal twenty-four-hour periods. That is, they believe Jesus's body must rest in the tomb a full seventy-two hours for His prophetic "sign of Jonah" prophecy to be fulfilled. But are they correct in this assumption? And does the Bible's claim to inerrancy really turn on this question? Let's take a closer look.

There are some problems with the view that Jesus spent a full seventy-two hours in the tomb. The first of these is those two passages in which we see Jesus mentioning "the sign of Jonah." They are Matthew 16:4 and Luke 11:29–32. Now, this reference to the "sign" in Matthew 16 is from a different occasion than the reference I mentioned earlier from Matthew 12. And there are differences between the two. In the later passage, Matthew 16:4, Jesus said:

> "A wicked and adulterous generation seeks for a sign, but no sign shall be given to it except the sign of the prophet Jonah." So He left them and departed.

If the period of time in the belly of the whale (or tomb) constituted the divine "sign," wouldn't Jesus have mentioned it here as well? The passage in Luke is even more illuminating. In Luke's account Jesus addresses not the scribes and Pharisees, but rather a crowd that is pressing in upon Him. To them He says, "This is an evil generation. It looks for a sign, but no sign will be given it except the sign of Jonah the prophet. *For as Jonah was a sign to the Ninevites, so will the Son of Man be to this generation*" (Luke 11:29–30, emphasis added).

Here the Savior makes it clear the "sign" was not a specific time period hidden away, but rather His appearance as a prophet carrying a message of repentance—a message punctuated and validated by a miraculous reappearance. Even so, we must still account for Jesus's use of the phrase "three days and three nights" in Matthew 12.

The answer comes easily once we understand the common idioms of language in Jesus's day—especially the way the phrase "a day and a night" was used in the rabbinic literature in that time. This phrase commonly applies to any portion of a day, rather than necessarily a full twenty-four-hour period. This is because, though it is hard for us to conceive, the ancients had no concept of *zero*. The emergence of zero as a number in and of itself took place in India more than eight centuries after Jesus's time. This had a subtle but profound impact on the way people counted sequences of things. Imagine playing baseball at a time in which nobody knows home plate exists. A base runner's *first* leg of his trip around the bases would land him on "second base" and his *second* leg would put him on "third base." This is essentially the way sequences were counted in Jesus's day.

This means that in biblical times, even the smallest portion of a day or of a night was reckoned as representing the whole day and night. This method of counting is sometimes called "inclusive reckoning." There are many examples of this type of counting, both in the Bible and in rabbinic writings from Jesus's era.

For example, 1 Samuel 30:12 describes an abandoned Egyptian servant who "had not eaten bread or drunk any water for three days and nights." In the very next verse this same servant states that his master had left him behind "three days ago." If the phrase "three days and three nights" *must* mean three twenty-four-hour periods, then the famished servant would have said he'd been abandoned *four* days before.

We find another very instructive example in Esther, one that connects to Jesus's use of the term in a key way. You may recall that when Queen Esther was tipped off by her uncle Mordecai about evil Haman's plot to exterminate the Jews of Persia, she responded with the following message: "Go, gather all the Jews who can be found in Susa, then fast for me. Stop eating and drinking for three days, night or day. I and my young women will fast likewise. Only then would I dare go to the king" (Esther 4:16).

Now, if delivery of Esther's message had required three full days and nights of fasting—that is a literal seventy-two-hour period—then she would have presented herself to King Ahasuerus on the *fourth* day. Yet we discover just a few verses later that Esther went before the king "on the third day" (Esther 5:1). These examples and others to which I could point clearly show that the "three days and three nights" was a common expression—one that is used in the Bible euphemistically to indicate not three whole twenty-four-hour days but rather three calendar days. Thus Esther's "three-day" fast could have consisted of the remaining hours of day one, all of day two, and a portion of day three leading up to her audience with the king. In terms of the Hebrew idiom, this sequence of events would have been perfectly consistent with her pledge to "stop eating and drinking for three days." This is the nature of inclusive reckoning.

It is significant that the Word of God states Esther appeared before the king "on the third day." Many of the Bible's statements concerning Jesus's death and resurrection use this same phrase. For example, the fifteenth chapter of 1 Corinthians is Paul's definitive declaration concerning the resurrection of Christ—affirming both its reality and its centrality to the gospel message. Early in that epic chapter, which we will explore in depth a little further on in our journey, Paul defines his gospel as this simple message: "that Christ died for our sins according to the Scriptures, and that He was buried, and that He *was raised on the third day* according to the Scriptures" (vv. 3–4, NAS, emphasis added).

Once again, this is Paul's unequivocal, emphatic, detailed treatise on the resurrection of Jesus Christ. He is taking great pains in this chapter to school—at length—the doubters, the confused, the skeptics, and the revisionists concerning Jesus's victory over death and the grave. The brilliant and learned rabbi formerly known as Saul of Tarsus could have easily said "*after* the third day" if that was what he meant. But there is no hint of "after" in the original Greek of Paul's statement. Every English translation I have ever encountered from the 1611 King James right down to the most recent modern renderings translate the phrase as either "on the third day" or simply "the third day."

Not to belabor the point, but if Jesus died on a Wednesday and spent three complete days and nights in the tomb, then He did not rise on the third day. He arose on the fourth.

We also know that throughout Jewish history and to this very day, rabbis have utilized the inclusive reckoning method to count the seven days required for "sitting shiva" upon the death of a family member or for scheduling circumcisions on the eighth day after the birth of a boy.[2]

Please permit me to call one final witness to the stand before we move forward to explore the wonders of the most exciting and significant event in all of human history. Among the first to see and speak with the risen Christ were the two disciples who, without recognition, encountered Him on the road to Emmaus. As we have already observed, the two had hightailed it out of Jerusalem the instant the Sabbath's travel restrictions expired.

In the twenty-fourth chapter of his Gospel, Luke begins by describing the Resurrection, opening with the words, "Now on the first day of the week, very early in the morning" (Luke 24:1). The first eight words of that sentence should eliminate all questions about what day the Savior emerged from the tomb. The first day of the week was and is Sunday. Later in the chapter, in introducing the Emmaus story, Luke writes, "Now *that same day* two of them were going" (v. 13, emphasis added). Again, our time frame is very clear.

Jesus, still unrecognized, asked them what they were talking about and why they seemed so despondent. They replied by describing the trial and the crucifixion of their trusted teacher and loving friend, Jesus of Nazareth. They spoke of their hopes that Jesus was about to redeem Israel from Roman oppression and how His death shattered those dreams. Then one of the two fleeing disciples said:

> Moreover, *today is the third day since these things happened.*
>
> —LUKE 24:21,
> EMPHASIS ADDED

These "things" are clearly the trial, crucifixion, and burial of their Lord. It is difficult to read any other meaning into this exchange other than that Jesus died on Friday and was seen alive on "the third day," that is, Sunday.

This was the sign of Jonah to that wicked and perverse generation. A man was swallowed up and assumed forever dead. But on the third day He miraculously reappeared with a prophetic message of hope: "Repent of your sins, and salvation is freely yours."

† † † † †

This was also a sign that everything had changed. Something had been weighed upon the cosmic scales of justice. A wrong had been righted. The earth had undergone some sort of regime change in a legal coup, and a vile, cruel dictator had been deposed. Let us pull back the dimensional curtain of time and watch that drama unfold.

We should return for a moment to the Garden of Eden. Before time began, the Ancient of Days stooped low, dipped His hands into the cold, red clay of earth, and crafted a man. The Master Artisan of the ages built the man a home and dwelt with him there in the opulent Garden of Eden. God and man were one.

In the brilliance of paradise, Adam fellowshipped freely with his Father. No reassurances were needed. Their relationship was one of reckless abandon. With the cool breezes of eternity blowing around man's shoulders, those words echoed in his mind: "Who shall separate me from the love of God?" But you know the story. Right there in the middle of a place called Abundance and Delight, Adam sided with God's great archenemy. A question seeded an act. And once bloomed, that act spawned a rebellion that dragged the entire human family into a voracious entrapment of degradation and defilement.

God came down, way down into the midst of all of that

betrayal. Man had wound his moral clock backward. The image of God had been dashed to pieces. The locust and its great king had come and turned blossom into dust. Death had come and turned blue the lips of the children of men.

With flaming sword, man was banished to the eastern plains of sterile Eden and there he stood in jeopardy before God and before the holy angels. Why? Because desire, when it conceives, produces sin. Sin, when it is finished, brings forth death. Man divorced himself, if you will, from divinity by refusing escape from the entanglements and enticements of evil.

Man engaged in a crazed conspiracy to become like God. His promise of the knowledge of good and evil was procured. Man suddenly became aware of every evil atrocity, sin, and abomination. Defiling knowledge flooded and filled his being, and with it, an acute awareness of everything good that lay just beyond his sin-infected reach.

In the quietness of that moment, he heard the words, "Only the pure in heart shall see God." But the pure had become polluted. Man had successfully separated himself from his Friend. A yawning chasm opened between Creator and creation. And in its darkened recesses, man began to devise a plan to satisfy sin's ceaseless cravings. You know that your Bible says there is a way to every one of us that seems right, but the end thereof is the way of death.

One exposure to Satan's corruption carried the communicable disease of sin, and it infiltrated into the bloodstream of all humanity. Earth became a graveyard planet. Lawlessness lorded over the land. Satan had separated man from his source of sustenance and substance, the life-infusing presence of God Himself. Man had missed the mark, fallen short. That's what sin is. He'd fallen short. Sin became the standard. Death became the decree, and God wept, because it was not His enemy, but His friend that had forsaken Him.

John Wesley, that great preacher from a bygone era, as a boy once asked his mother, "Mother, what is sin?" Isn't that the riveting question today? What is black enough, what is cold enough, what is strong enough to separate you from a loving God? What is strong enough to pry you out of the unyielding hands of a caring and compassionate Creator? Sin and sin alone. "What is it?" Wesley asked his mother. Her sage answer was, "Whatever weakens your reason, impairs the tenderness of your conscience, obscures your sense of God, and takes off the relish of spiritual things—that to you is sin."[3]

But we can't end the story there. We have to go way, way back. Man sinned in that garden. God separated him from the tree of life so that he would not live in that fallen state forever. Thus his banishment from that garden was actually an act of mercy! But look at man now.

Behold man! The furrow in his brow spoke of the agony that rode across his face. No happy, laughing, splashing river of life—instead, a river of tears. Man's only hope? To dig holes in the ground and bury his children. The earth was walled all about with great wooden gates and iron bands, and there was no way out—except, that is, for Genesis chapter three, where God made a propitiation, a promise with hope attached.

God said (and I paraphrase), "It may not happen tomorrow, and it may not happen a year from now, but there will come One, the Seed planted in the forest of eternity, entwining its roots around the Rock of Ages. And concerning that Seed, Satan, you will bruise His heel, but He will crush your head."

Mercy climbed up in its chariot and rode up to the gates of justice and the law, and pounded on them and said, "Let me in!" Mercy said, "If you'll let me in, I'll come in, and I'll wipe those fevered brows. I'll mop those sweaty palms. I'll lift up those hanging heads. I'll raise up those weighted hearts." But Justice and the Law said, "No, sir! No one from time can unlock these bands, swing wide these gates, and open a corridor. That will take someone from eternity."

So Mercy said, "I'll fix that." Mercy jumped back up in his chariot, slapped the lathered sides of that steed, and pulled up into the gates of glory. He rode high up on the forever mountain, scooped up the Living Son of God, put Him in his chariot, rode down through the corridors of time and space, past the Milky Way, past the planets, spinning and whirling, for a stop on this blue marble planet.

Jesus walked out of Mercy's chariot, walked up to the gates of Justice and the Law and said, "Let Me in."

Justice said, "No, sir. There must be a price paid."

Jesus said, "Name the price."

"For their misery, joy. For their death, life. There must be bloodshed sufficient enough to heal the wounding sin and putrefying sores of humanity." At this answer, Jesus grabbed Justice by the nape of the neck, jerked him up in front of that gate, and said, "I'll make the payment."

With a trembling voice, Justice asked, "When can we expect payment, Sir?"

And Jesus said, "Four thousand years hence, you meet Me in the middle of this cemetery planet, and I'll pay the price in full."

You know the rest of the story. Our Canaan King came conquering and to conquer, riding in dyed garments of Bozrah, riding on the strength of His own might. In a Bethlehem barn He burst through the flanks of that little fourteen-year-old virgin girl, born in a manger. That's where a lamb ought to be born. For thirty-three and one-half years He walked on this planet and displayed mastery over demons, depravity, and disease, and at the tomb of Lazarus, even over Death itself! First in Nain's streets, then in the burial place of Bethany, He manifested His strength over Death.

But look at Him now. They'd kicked and prodded Him

through the cobblestone streets of Jerusalem. An entire detachment of Roman soldiers had beaten Him until His own mother did not recognize Him. See Him writhing in His own blood. See the scarlet river by which the very veins of God Himself were emptied. Watch blood run down a naked side and drip off His toes into bloody pools upon the very same earth He Himself had created all those millennia ago.

Watch them lift up to Him vinegar and gall to drink. He cried, "I thirst," and then those words, "*Eli, Eli, lama sabachthani.* My Father and my God, why have you forsaken me?" As Psalm 18 reveals, the Father God doubled His fist and smote His own Son on that rugged and cruel beam. Then, He turned away. God, who carpets the valley in green—God, who feeds the baby raven—turned His back on His Son.

He died alone. Up again and down again on nail-pierced feet and hands until finally He said, "It is finished. Father, into Thy hands I commit My spirit." Then your Bible says He gave up the ghost. Your Bible does not say that Jesus's Spirit died, only that the earthly tabernacle that housed it expired on that hill. When He said, "It is finished," I can tell you His Spirit shouted, "It has only just begun!" The Spirit of Jesus Christ jumped off that cross, riding at the summit of Calvary.

Death itself—with its sickle, its caped head, and its stronghold filled with skulls, bones, dust, moth, and corruption— rode back and forth on that pus-colored horse, slapping its lathered sides with its reins, and said, "I do not fear any Son of Man. I've never lost a battle. You mean to tell me that is the best heaven had to offer? Do you mean to tell me," Death said, "that is who they sent to war with me—that puny, wheezing, bleeding, mumbling specimen?"

Death raced up the sides of Calvary, intending to scoop up the body of Jesus, put Him in a tomb somewhere, and that would be the end of it. Holiness would never be reintroduced to the earth, and sin would rule the darkened hearts of men forever! But about halfway up that hillside, your Bible says the real Jesus leaped off that cross. He went chasing Death for three days. He chased him through every graveyard in Jerusalem. He chased him all about Capernaum. He chased him into the very corridors of hell, and there He put one foot on its devil hordes and the other on the crumbling empire of Death, raised His hands to the Father, and shouted, "I am Alpha and Omega! I am the resurrection! I am the life!"

He cornered the devil in his throne room, perched on that putrid throne of skulls and bones. Satan warned, "Don't come one step further."

Jesus replied, "Listen, foul deceiver, let me explain something to you. If the lions were no match for Daniel, your skulls and bones are no match for Life. I am the Way! I am the Truth! I am the Life!"

Then He snatched the keys of death, hell, and the grave from the gnarled hands of the Antichrist, locked them to the wheels of His chariot, and went riding across the sunbaked walls of the devil's perdition, singing, "Free at last, free at last! Thank God Almighty! We're free at last!"

That victory shout triggered an earthquake that shook all Sheol. The tremor then rumbled upward, upward until it rolled through the Judean hills. The epicenter was a garden cemetery outside of the walls of Jerusalem. Numerous graves around the city split open and the occupants rose up to be reunited with their astonished loved ones.

He shouted once more, this time to the jubilant millions of righteous dead inhabiting Paradise. "Follow Me, My patient brothers! This place is no longer your home. The seed of the woman has crushed that old serpent's head. We're going to see the Father. And I must sprinkle My blood upon the mercy seat there in heaven's holy of holies."

Then mankind's victorious Champion looked up and saw a shaft of light piercing the thick darkness of the underworld. A luminous angel had tossed a massive sealing stone aside as if it were made of paper.

PART III:

SUNDAY

Chapter 6

HE IS NOT HERE

Tomb, thou shalt not hold Him longer;
Death is strong, but Life is stronger;
Stronger than the dark, the light;
Stronger than the wrong, the right.
Faith and Hope triumphant say,
Christ will rise on Easter-Day.[1]

> ▸ PHILLIPS BROOKS
> (1835–1893)

H IS BODY, SWADDLED in grave clothes, was laid in a borrowed tomb. Inside, it was utterly dark and unspeakably still. Outside, the Roman guards, in the midst
of what was quite literally a graveyard shift, had built a small
fire to fend off the encroaching chill of the Judean night. For
stretches of time they were silent, staring into the embers and
thinking of home, yet they conversed periodically to help keep
one another awake. Be assured, there would be no sleeping on
guard duty that night, or on any other night for that matter.
Doing so was punishable by death in the same manner as that
suffered by the Nazarene corpse over which they now stood

watch: crucifixion. No, these men would find ways to remain awake through the night, even if it required jabbing each other with their javelins.

As for the disciples, they remained in hiding, certain they would be arrested, tried, and executed the moment they were spotted in public. Nothing consumes the thoughts and the mind like seeing your seemingly invincible leader tortured to death. Only days earlier He had seemed so fierce—working miracles, turning over tables and boldly rebuking the corrupt religious establishment's leaders. Then suddenly everything changed on Thursday night. There was that somber meal together, the talk of being betrayed, and the anguished, late night prayer vigil over on the Mount of Olives. When Judas and the temple soldiers arrived later that evening, the disciples all expected a fight, or at least some sort of standoff. Instead Jesus had meekly allowed Himself to be led away like a lamb to the slaughter. It was all so shockingly different than what they had expected.

The eleven, along with a number of other followers, had probably separated into two or possibly three clusters. One group most likely huddled at the Jerusalem residence of James and John. Peter was among these. So were the women who had witnessed the crucifixion and assisted with the hasty burial— Mary Magdalene, Mary (mother of James and Joses, wife of Clopas), Salome (mother of James and John, wife of Zebedee), and Joanna.

Another group had likely retreated to nearby Bethany where Mary, Martha, and resurrected Lazarus resided. Finally, we know that two disciples from one of these groups were planning to leave at first light for the relative safety of Emmaus.

Now that the Sabbath had ended, Mary Magdalene and several of the other women planned to rise before dawn and make their way back to the tomb. Compounding the grief and shock they felt at the events of the last forty-eight hours was the knowledge that the normally detailed and time-consuming Jewish burial rituals were rushed and not done adequately for the One they loved so dearly. They ministered to Him in life and were now nearly frantic to demonstrate the same devotion in death.

As these women attempted to sleep, they had no idea a Roman guard now stood directly outside the tomb. They could not be aware that the official seal of the Roman prefect upon that stone had, for all intents and purposes, made access to the body impossible.

Here at the midnight hour, in the darkest part of the darkest day the earth has ever seen, it seemed everyone was waiting. The soldiers waited for the watch to pass and their relief to arrive. The disciples waited in trembling dread of pounding at the door. And the women who loved the Savior waited for the night hours to pass so they could resume their burial ministrations.

Others waited as well. Unseen, all of heaven's myriad hosts—angels, archangels, seraphim, cherubim, and living creatures with six wings and eyes all around—kept a hushed vigil. Hell's denizens waited and watched, too. So did a groaning, curse-ravaged earth. Indeed, all of creation waited breathlessly to know the answer to a single question: Would God veto the crucifixion with a resurrection?

As it turned out, hell was the first to know.

It began with the creaking and groaning of ancient metal on metal, as the King of Glory lifted the gates of damnation off their rusty hinges, flung them aside, and waded through the layered ashes of bygone millennia. With one hand, He gripped a ring of primeval keys. The other hand He lifted heavenward to the Father, and He shouted in a voice that rolled like thunder through labyrinthine halls of Hades and dwelling places of Paradise:

> Do not be afraid. I am the First and the Last. I am He who lives, though I was dead. Look! I am alive forever-more. Amen. And I have the keys of Hades and of Death.
> —REVELATION 1:17–18

"You'll have to excuse Me now," He continued as He looked upward. "I have an appointment, and I must not be late."

Far above Him, the stillness of the chilly night was suddenly roiled by an earthquake. For the Roman soldiers, the smooth, familiar monotony and boredom of overnight guard duty instantly shattered into a thousand little pieces of alarm and confusion. Concurrent with the earthquake, a flash of radiant light erupted within the tomb and shot out from around the edges of the massive sealing stone, momentarily bathing the garden in brilliance like that of a lightning flash. Then the whole area was illuminated once more as two massive men dressed in blinding white suddenly appeared before them.

The moment the earth began to move, the soldiers instinctively unsheathed their broad Roman swords. But those weapons clanged and clattered on the stony ground as they were dropped by hardened, seasoned fighting men experiencing a deeper terror than any they had ever known in their lives. They staggered backward and fell to the ground, unable to speak, or even move, much less run away. The paralyzed soldiers stared dumbfounded as one of the magnificent beings in white extended two fingers and with a flick of his wrist rolled the stone away and took a seat upon it.

What they saw next caused them to faint away like dead men. On the third day, the removal of the *golel* revealed a man standing in the opening of the sepulchre.

He arose in the dark. Our familiar Easter sunrise services have trained us to associate the Resurrection with sunrise. This is because the discovery of the empty tomb by the women occurred around daybreak. All four Gospels record their arrival at the tomb at or just before sunrise on the day after the Sabbath. As Mark describes it, "Very early in the morning, on the first day of the week, they came to the tomb at the rising of the sun" (Mark 16:2).

This means they assembled and began their journey to the garden while it was still quite dark. When they arrived, as every Sunday school child can tell you, the tomb was already quite empty.

So, I emphasize this once more. He arose in the dark. There is a large message in this small detail of the Resurrection narrative.

We ought not wait for our circumstances to brighten to put our hope in a faithful God. We must not say to God, "Show me some improvement and then I'll believe in Your goodness and mercy." No, it is when things seem the most hopeless and grim that we should anchor our faith to the rock of expectancy. It is when it seems "too late" that we must muster words of praise and thanksgiving.

We all recall that Paul and Silas sang a hymn of praise from the depths of a filthy Philippian dungeon, but do we remember when? I summon Acts 16:25 to rise and testify. "At midnight Paul and Silas were praying and singing hymns to God." When did these fettered saints find their song of praise? At midnight! When things seemed the most hopeless! You know the result. "Suddenly there was a great earthquake, so that the foundations of the prison were shaken. And immediately all the doors were opened and everyone's shackles were loosened" (Acts 16:26).

I encourage you not to wait on the dawn to find your shout of confidence in God. Remember, your greatest opposition always comes at the point of your breakthrough. So sing your song now, in the middle of your midnight hour, when trouble seems to be pressing in all around you. Anyone can sing God's praise on a clear day at noon. That kind of faith doesn't alarm principalities and powers.

The day doesn't begin at dawn. It begins at midnight. Likewise, that is when God's resurrection power comes. Tombs open in the middle of the night. Graves burst open in the middle of the night. Jesus comes walking on the waves in the middle of the night with a message for you and me. It is that very one He spoke to Jairus, who had just absorbed the news that his daughter had died: "Do not fear. Only believe" (Luke 8:50).

Don't be afraid of the dark.

Your Bible says they began before dawn. These women who loved their Savior so arose and made their way back to the place where He lay. The full paschal moon that had illuminated the Garden of Gethsemane just a few nights past was diminished in brightness only a little, and thus lighted the first steps of their journey back to the borrowed tomb of Jesus. When they arrived, the rim of the eastern sky was a brightening pink.

Each woman was heavy of heart but also heavy laden with the materials necessary for their work—fragrant oils, aloes, myrrh, and other spices, along with fresh linen wrappings. Along the way they discussed the principle obstacle to carrying out their mission, namely, that enormous stone the men had struggled to roll into place across the entrance to the sepulchre. There had been a gardener, Mary Magdalene recalled. Perhaps he would be there. Maybe he would enlist some help. In other words, they went with no guarantee of access. Faith, hope, and love alone drew them to the garden where they had laid Jesus's shattered body.

When the group finally reached the garden, they were shocked to find the stone rolled away and the tomb seemingly empty. Mary Magdalene jumped to a conclusion. She presumed the same hateful, jealous religious leaders who lobbied for the Master's execution had come in the night and taken control of His body. "Who knows what additional horrors and humiliations they have planned for Him," she thought. "Do they plan to put His lifeless body on display somewhere?" She couldn't bear the thought, so she immediately fled the garden and ran directly back to Peter and John to report:

> So she came running to Simon Peter and to the other disciple whom Jesus loved, and said to them, "They have taken the Lord out of the tomb, and we do not know where they have put Him."
>
> —JOHN 20:2

The remaining women in the garden investigated. Entering the tomb, at first they found it empty. Suddenly two men in luminous robes appeared before their astonished eyes. The startled mourners bowed in fear and awe. Then they heard these words from one of the men:

> Why do you seek the living among the dead? He is not here, but has risen! Remember how He spoke to you while He was still in Galilee, saying, "The Son of Man must be delivered into the hands of sinful men, and be crucified, and on the third day rise again."
>
> —LUKE 24:5–7

Yes! Of course! He had indeed said those very words! A surge of remembrance now flowed like a rushing river. They hurried back to the disciples' safe house to report what they had seen and heard.

Of course, Mary Magdalene had a significant head start. She reached the place where Peter and John were hiding and breathlessly related her fears concerning the fate of Jesus's body. Without hesitation, both men charged the exit door. John, being significantly younger than the impulsive fisherman, made much better time and reached the garden first. He saw the dislodged sealing stone just as Mary described it.

He prepared to enter the tomb, but a wave of trepidation washed over him. "Is this an ambush?" Suddenly it seemed like a wonderful idea to wait for Peter to arrive. So, instead of entering the tomb, he stood in the doorway and slowly leaned in as far as he could. His eyes strained in the dimness, but he was able to discern only the flattened outlines of grave clothes lying on the stone shelf where the body should have been. And he couldn't see a body in any other portion of the tomb within his line of sight.

Eventually Peter arrived, out of breath and soaked with sweat. When he recovered sufficiently, he ducked down and entered the sepulchre. He too noted the body wrappings on the shelf and also saw the head wrap, or napkin, lying elsewhere. He made the same assumption that Mary Magdalene had, perhaps because she had already planted the thought in his mind. "Someone has taken Jesus's body."

When John put these events to paper years later in the Gospel that bears his name, instead of referring to himself by name he called himself "the other disciple." In the telling, he mentioned a small but extraordinary detail in his narrative of that morning. Read carefully the words of John's eyewitness account:

Then Simon Peter came, following him, and went inside the tomb. He saw the linen cloths lying there, and the cloth that was around His head, *not lying with the linen cloths, but wrapped in a place by itself.* Then the other disciple, who came first to the tomb, went in also. *He saw and believed.*

—JOHN 20:6–8,
EMPHASIS ADDED

John, the eyewitness, went to extraordinary lengths in this passage to make sure we understand the exact arrangement of the grave clothes here. What did he see that provoked him to belief? Could he have noticed something the others, in their hurry and distress, missed? I believe he did.

John scanned the details in the tomb much as a detective would view a crime scene. He paid attention to detail and allowed the things he saw to tell the story of what had taken place there. In just a few seconds, clever John was able to evaluate the available evidence and draw some logically sound conclusions.

First, he reasoned that if someone were going to steal the body, there would be no reason to remove the burial wrappings and leave them behind. It would have been far faster, simpler, and more conducive to transporting the body to simply grab it and go. No, the evidence did not suggest theft of the body. But there was something else about the position and condition of the burial wrappings that called out to John.

You will recall that Jesus's body was wrapped quickly but tightly in multiple layers of linen cloth interspersed with layers of sticky, perfumed oils and waxes. You will also recall that the head was wrapped separately with the "napkin." The fact is, after roughly thirty-six hours in the cool, dry Judean air of that tomb, the wax-soaked linens would have adhered to the body like glue and already begun to harden into a shell. The only effective way to remove that body from those wrappings would have been to cut it out.

It is clear that what John saw was not the random, messy pile of cloth strips one would expect if someone had unwound them or if Jesus had revived in the tomb and then somehow managed to free Himself. No, what John saw was the wrappings still in the form of the body. That is, the grave wrappings were intact and in the actual shape in which they had been wound around Jesus's body, only flattened, as if someone had let the air out of a balloon!

Other evidence spoke to John. He saw the napkin neatly folded in another corner of the tomb. Someone had taken the time to calmly and methodically fold this sheet of linen and place it, just so. No grave robber would do this. But he knew well someone who would.

John surveyed this scene and realized only one possible explanation fit the evidence at hand. The undisturbed grave clothes demonstrated that Jesus had risen through and out of them. His body passed through the winding strips of linen—just as it would later pass through locked and barred doors—leaving them completely intact. Jesus's body had not only been reanimated by the power and life of Almighty God, it had been transformed into a glorified heavenly body—the type every believer in Him will one day receive!

Ever impatient, Peter was not there to witness John's epiphany. He had already headed back to their base. Perhaps his assumption that the body had been stolen further heightened his paranoia about being arrested. John, on the other hand, lingered there and took in the scene just a moment longer. Standing in the streaks of golden sunlight now piercing the darkness of the sepulchre, John stared at the neatly folded napkin. A smile slowly spread across his face. This disciple whom Jesus loved "saw and believed."

✝ ✝ ✝ ✝ ✝

I have visited the Garden Tomb in Jerusalem on more than one occasion. As I have already suggested, we cannot know with absolute certainty that this specific tomb is the one in which Jesus was laid. It is very possible, however, that it is. Even if it is not, we can be sure that it is very much like it in every respect. It is in the right place and of the right era. It fits the biblical descriptions in every aspect.

Inside, at the end of the shelf carved out for the body, there is a niche for the feet. It is as if the stonemasons knew that the person who would be laid there would be six inches too tall to fit on the shelf. I vividly recall one particular visit to that remarkable cave-like space. In awe and gratitude, I placed my hand inside that niche and thought about those precious nail-riven feet that may have rested there for a few hours.

As I turned and prepared to step back out into that brilliant Israeli daylight, I heard the familiar voice of my Savior whisper to my spirit man. If I live to be one hundred I will not forget that spot on which I stood or what I heard Him say in that moment. Ever so sweetly, the Master said, "Tell them I'm coming."

I will obey that command right now and tell you, it's true. He's coming back on the clouds of glory. He's coming again. He told me so. A herald angel told the astonished disciples the same thing just after they saw Him soar up into the sky and disappear in the clouds. "Men of Galilee," he had said, "why stand looking toward heaven? This same Jesus, who was taken up from you to heaven, will come in like manner as you saw Him go into heaven" (Acts 1:11).

When I ponder His promise to return, I cannot help thinking about that folded napkin in the tomb. Of course, it serves as a silent but powerful refutation of any claim that the body of

Jesus was stolen from the tomb, but perhaps it is telling us something more.

A Roman-era tradition concerns another type of napkin, the kind used by the head of the wealthy household when reclining at dinner. It seems the napkin could be used as a signal to the serving staff. According to this tradition, a carelessly wadded napkin when leaving the table meant, "I am finished with this meal. I will not be returning." But if the master folded his napkin and laid it beside his plate when getting up from the table, this was a sign to his servants that said, "I'm not finished yet." In other words, the folded napkin meant, "I'm coming back!"

We, the devoted servants of Jesus Christ, don't have to guess or speculate as to whether or not He will be returning. We have this extraordinary promise directly from His gracious lips:

> Let not your heart be troubled. You believe in God. Believe also in Me. In My Father's house are many dwelling places. If it were not so, I would have told you. I am going to prepare a place for you. And if I go and prepare a place for you, I will come again and receive you to Myself, that where I am, you may be also.
>
> —JOHN 14:1–3

He *is* coming back. He told me to tell you this. And I can't wait to hear the sound of the trumpet blast and meet Him in the air when He splits the eastern sky. Faster than the fleetest hoof that ever struck pavement or a wheel ever turned on an axle, He's coming back! Like lightning out of a dark-throated storm cloud, Jesus is coming again. He's coming back for you and for me!

† † † † †

Mary Magdalene's report to Peter and John had sent the men racing toward the tomb. She had wept uncontrollably at the thought of His body going unburied. We have seen what a horrifying prospect such a fate presented to the first-century Jewish mind. She knew nothing of what the other women saw and heard inside the sepulchre. They had run to one or more of the other safe houses.

Now, after several minutes of collecting herself, she decided to join the men back at the tomb, but by the time she arrived, the two disciples had already left. At the sight of the open cave Mary's tears began flowing once more. She had half-hoped it had been a dream. Seeing no sign of the men in the garden or the outer courtyard of the tomb, she stooped down to look inside.

Mary was startled at the sight of the same two men the other women had encountered. Through tear-filled and swollen eyes she saw them sitting at either end of the shelf upon which Jesus's body had been laid. This was precisely where the other women had seen them.

"Woman, why are you weeping?" asked one of the men in robes of whitest white.

"Because they have taken away my Lord, and I do not know where they have put Him," she sobbed.

At this point we must pause and wonder why Peter and John, who were just there moments before, did not see these men. Either the angels had been there the whole time and the men were simply not granted eyes to see them, or the heavenly sentinels deliberately departed during the time these two were inside the tomb. In either event, only women have been granted a supernatural angelic announcement this morning. Only the women who loved and served Jesus have been directly told the stunning truth. *He lives.*

It seems as if heaven is deliberately arranging circumstances so that the eleven remaining disciples will only hear of Jesus's resurrection from the mouths of other mortals. With the possible exception of John, these will uniformly greet the news these various women deliver to them with skepticism or outright disbelief. Thomas was far from the only doubter in Jesus's inner circle.

Ultimately Jesus will appear to them and they will believe. They will see and feel the nail prints in His hands. They will note His spear-violated side. They will dine on roasted fish and bread with Him. Then, in their final meetings with their risen friend and Lord, He will commission them to go into all the world and proclaim Him crucified, risen, and alive forevermore. He will ask them to ask others to believe these things with nothing more than the word of their testimony. In other words, He will ask them to help others do what they could not do because the Holy Spirit had not yet been sent.

They will ultimately recall that priestly prayer He had prayed the night He was arrested. He had prayed specifically for them, His disciples, but He'd reached further in His intercession. "I do not pray for these alone, but also for those who will believe in Me through their word," He had said (John 17:20). Perhaps the disciples were denied the angelic announcement precisely because it would soon be their task to deliver the good news to unbelievers who would have nothing to go on but their witness and an inward pull from the Spirit of God. Then this gospel must spread across the world and across the centuries in precisely this same way—that is, through the telling by simple people of a simple story. A loving God became man, walked among us living a sinless life, died for our sins, and rose on the third day.

The inherent irony of this was not lost on Augustine, who once wrote, "What courteous consideration on His part, to have granted us the power to believe what we cannot yet see! We believe the words of those who, at first, did not believe their own eyes."[2]

For on this first Resurrection Sunday morning, only women have heard and believed. Turning to exit the tomb, the heart-broken Mary Magdalene noticed a third man in white standing just outside the entrance. Due to the low height of the tomb's opening she could only see the figure from the chest down. "Here is that gardener whose help I had hoped to enlist in the removal of the stone," she assumed. "Maybe he saw something." She approached the man but, in accordance with Jewish customs of the day, did not make eye contact. Before she could pose her question, this man had two for her.

"Woman, why are you weeping? Whom are you seeking?"

"Sir, if You have carried Him away, tell me where You have put Him, and I will take Him away."

At this, the stranger said one word that instantly changed everything—her disposition, her assumptions, her theology—indeed it changed every moment of the rest of her life. That single word was her name.

"Mary," He said.

That voice! That tone! No one said her name like He did. No one could communicate both love and authority in fullest measure the way He could. He said her name that way the day He'd set her free from a lifetime of shame and torment. Now, the mere voicing of her name freed her from pain and confusion. A shattered heart was made whole in an instant.

She ran to embrace Him, but He gently backed away. She was separated from Him by death. Now she expressed her earnest desire to never be apart from Him again by falling to her knees and holding on to Him. But truly His resurrection had changed everything. He lovingly remonstrated her. "Stop holding on to Me," He said, "for I have not yet ascended to My Father. But go to My brothers and tell them, 'I am ascending to My Father and your Father, to My God and your God'" (John 20:17).

What was the significance of ascending to His Father? An understanding of the ancient Yom Kippur (Day of Atonement) ritual, instituted by Moses at God's own command, provides our answer.

As stipulated in the sixteenth chapter of Leviticus, once a year, on the Day of Atonement, the high priest would make sacrifices for himself, the nation, and the priesthood. He would fill the holy of holies with smoke from the altar of incense, and there, standing in the awesome shekinah presence of the God Most High, sprinkle the blood of the sacrifice on the mercy seat of the ark of the covenant so the sins of the people would be covered for another year.

Before performing these vital, holy duties, the high priest would thoroughly wash and cleanse himself. He would then meticulously avoid touching anything unclean or defiling before entering the holy of holies.

In the eighth chapter of Hebrews, we learn that the earthly tabernacle of Moses—its shape, layout, and furnishings—was built in accordance with a pattern shown to Moses. That pattern was the very dwelling place of God in heaven. The earthly priests "serve in a sanctuary that is an example and shadow of the heavenly one" (Heb. 8:5). In other words, the earthly holy of holies in the original tabernacle and later in the magnificent temples of Solomon and Herod were merely crude copies of a place in the heart of heaven.

One chapter later in Hebrews we learn that at some point following His death and resurrection, Jesus entered that true, original holy of holies in heaven, where His redeeming and cleansing sacrifice provided a pardon that could have never been achieved with animal sacrifices:

> But Christ, when He came as a High Priest of the good things to come, by a greater and more perfect tabernacle, not made with hands, that is to say, not of this creation, neither by the blood of goats and calves, but by His own blood, He entered the Most Holy Place once for all, having obtained eternal redemption.
>
> —HEBREWS 9:11–12

Jesus, our magnificent once-and-for-all High Priest, having performed a once-and-for-all Day of Atonement sacrifice, and having walked through the purifying fire of obedience unto death, would soon enter that heavenly holy place.

Having fully prepared Himself, He strode into the very throne room of God Himself, stepped up to the heavenly mercy seat, and was accepted by the Supreme Judge and Ruler of the universe on the merit of His sinless sacrifice on the altar of the cross.

But why did He tell Mary not to hold on to Him? It was not that He risked being defiled by unclean humanity. He walked among and touched lepers and others who were unclean with all manner of contagious diseases during His miraculous ministry and did not avoid any of them. How much more, after His resurrection, would He be untroubled by the devotion of someone so dear to Him? Besides, later on that same day others touched Him without restriction.

The answer lies in a further examination of what Mary did, and what Jesus commissioned her to do. She did not just touch Him, as in making contact with Him—she held Him, or as other translations render it, she clung to Him. His intention was to send her as a witness to those who did not yet believe He had risen. At the same time, He had other tasks to fulfill, which required His presence elsewhere. Eventually, He would ascend to the Father, and she, and all those who trusted Him as Savior, would know Him in a different way than they ever had before. No longer would His disciples rely on His physical presence, but they would depend on a knowing that surpassed their senses. Paul explained it this way in 2 Corinthians 5:16: "Yes, though we have known Christ according to the flesh, yet we do not regard Him as such from now on."

God indeed vetoed the Crucifixion with the Resurrection for "it was not possible that He should be held by it [death]" (Acts 2:24). This became an unanswerable demonstration of the central fact concerning Jesus of Nazareth. It is a fact unsearchable in its profundity and implications, yet it is so simple a five-year-old child can grasp it. That fact is, He lives.

He lives! The British evangelist G. Campbell Morgan found three key messages in the Savior's emergence from that dark tomb that Sunday morning:

> The value of the resurrection as a Divine act, is three-fold. First it is God's attestation of the perfection of the life of the Man Jesus. Secondly it is God's attestation of the perfection of the mediation of the Saviour Jesus. Thirdly it is God's attestation of the perfection of the victory of the King Jesus.[3]

Christianity is the only faith on earth with a virgin womb at one end and an empty tomb at the other. He is not here. He is risen, as He said.

Chapter 7

BELIEVING

It was the signed manual of the Deity, it was the seal of the Sovereign of the Universe affixed to His claim, it declared Him to be all that He had ever professed to be, and so it establishes the truth of all His teachings... The great fact that Jesus Christ rose from the dead is the central fact of the evidence of Christianity.[1]

> ➤ JOHN A. BROADUS
> (1827–1895)

BEYOND THE STONE walls of the garden, over in crowded Jerusalem, much was transpiring. Four Roman soldiers had recovered sufficiently from an overnight encounter with the resurrection power of God to make their way to the chief priests and report their experience.

This was a revealing moment for Caiaphas, the other priests, and all the elders of the nation. They assembled in council to hear the testimony of the soldiers. Keep in mind that these were not Jesus followers testifying at these proceedings. These men were not even Jewish. These were Roman soldiers with no interest in either side of the issue. They simply reported what they saw and heard. In the middle of the night, there was an earthquake. There were also luminous beings, one of whom who had "a countenance like lightning" and single-handedly moved a stone that had required many men to put in place.

Upon hearing these things, any person possessing a shred of intellectual honesty or spiritual integrity would have paused to wonder if perhaps the claims of the miracle worker from Galilee might actually be true. After all, the very reason they had arranged for the guard in the first place was that the Galilean had predicted He would rise on the third day. Now here it was that third day, and battle-hardened Roman soldiers were standing before them swearing that inexplicable events had paralyzed them with terror and resulted in the revival and departure of the formerly "dead" man.

This was clearly a moment to repent in sackcloth and ashes before God, pleading for His mercy for being hard hearted, prideful, and blind. If not that, then at least it was time to have the humility to say, "You know, we may have been wrong about this man we rejected, mocked, and finally silenced by His tyrannical and callous death upon a cross. Yet something remarkable, even supernatural, has clearly happened here. Let us pause to see how this plays out." But these men refused to respond in these ways. As Matthew reports:

> When the chief priests were assembled with the elders and had taken counsel, they gave much money to the soldiers, saying, "You are to say, 'His disciples came by night and stole Him away while we were sleeping.' If this comes to the governor's ears, we will satisfy him and keep you secure." So they took the money and did as they were instructed. And this saying has been commonly reported among the Jews to this day.
>
> —MATTHEW 28:12–15

How dark must a man's soul be for him to learn he may very well have participated in crucifying the Son of God, Israel's Messiah, and yet persist in promulgating a lie? Such a heart must be hard and cold beyond belief.

Meanwhile, in keeping with the "ladies first" theme of the day, Jesus appeared to the other women who had seen the angels at the empty tomb and heard the heavenly announcement.

> As they went to tell His disciples, suddenly Jesus met them, saying, "Greetings!" They came and took hold of His feet and worshipped Him. Then Jesus said to them, "Do not be afraid. Go tell My brothers to go to Galilee, and there they will see Me."
> —MATTHEW 28:9–10

These women were probably on their way to Bethany, the most likely location of the disciples who were not with John in Jerusalem. When they arrived, their astonishing story of the angelic announcement at the tomb and their subsequent encounter with the risen Savior Himself on the road was met with skepticism and outright disbelief. Nevertheless the disciples there headed for Jerusalem to reunite with John, Peter, and any other disciples staying there.

Meanwhile, Jesus made His next appearance, this time with the two men now making their way to Emmaus. We know the name of only one of these disciples. It is Cleopas. Neither was a member of Jesus's inner circle of twelve.

Whoever these disciples were, they suddenly found themselves joined on the road by a stranger. It was the risen Jesus, but Luke's account informs us "their eyes were kept from recognizing Him" (Luke 24:16). As we observed in chapter 5, He asked them what they were talking about and the cause of their obvious sadness. They recounted the events of the past few days and concluded with the startling news they had heard just as they were leaving Jerusalem shortly after daybreak. They related that some of their women had gone to the tomb before sunrise and found it empty.

"They returned saying that they had even seen a vision of angels, who said that He was alive" (Luke 24:23).

Notice that the women's direct encounter with angels at the tomb had now become a "vision" in these men's retelling. They then mentioned Peter and John's trip to the tomb, and that they too had found it empty.

Jesus responded to their answer with a fairly direct rebuke:

> O fools! And slow of heart to believe what the prophets
> have spoken! Was it not necessary for the Christ to suffer
> these things and to enter His glory?
> —LUKE 24:25–26

Why this stern response from the still-unrecognized Jesus? It is because the men's very presence on the road revealed they didn't believe a word of what they had heard that morning. If they had believed there was even the slightest possibility that what those women said they'd seen and heard was true, they would not have thought of leaving the city.

From this point forward Jesus took control of the conversation and cited scripture after scripture that pointed to the events they had just been describing. He took them on a whirlwind tour of the Old Testament, revealing the multitude of ways the Messiah's death and resurrection had been prophetically inevitable and utterly foreseeable.

They then stopped at a village for a meal. Jesus took some bread, spoke a blessing over it, broke it, and handed them each a piece. Something about His words and mannerisms in this act of bread breaking were uncannily familiar to the two men. Suddenly the scales fell from their eyes. Recognition flooded their souls. And in that instant He vanished before their blinking eyes.

The two men rushed back to Jerusalem where the disciples were gathering to discuss the day's events. In the meantime, we know that Jesus appeared to Peter alone, although the Bible did not record the details of that encounter.

Mark's Gospel is succinct and unflinching in describing the atmosphere of unbelief that permeated the room in which the rest of the disciples had gathered. When a euphoric Mary Magdalene returned to tell of having touched and spoken with the Master, Mark flatly stated, "they did not believe it" (Mark 16:11). When Cleopas and his traveling companion arrived back in Jerusalem, they too reported their encounter to ten disciples gathered there. The Emmaus men told their breathless and ecstatic story of how "their hearts burned within them" as Jesus cited the Scriptures and how they had ultimately come to recognize Him. They described how He had simply vanished before their astonished eyes. This remarkable testimony from not one but two reliable eyewitnesses hit an equally thick wall of skepticism in that room. Mark bluntly says of the two travelers, "And they went and told it to the rest, but they did not believe them either" (v. 13).

It would require repeated direct appearances to break through that wall of doubt. That wall would, however, ultimately crumble. Jesus would pass through locked doors and appear and disappear at will. They would touch Him. They would eat meals with Him. They would reminisce with Him of times past and receive instruction for the future.

Years later, the physician-historian Luke wrote to his dear friend Theophilus about this season of time for the eleven. He described the disciples as being those "to whom He presented Himself alive after His passion *by many infallible proofs,* appearing to them for forty days, and speaking concerning the kingdom of God" (Acts 1:3, emphasis added).

Here is the vital point to grasp in all of this. The clear witness of Scripture is that this was a group of men thoroughly predisposed to *disbelieve* in the Resurrection. These minds and hearts did not leap to assume He was alive at the first hint of that possibility. On the contrary, these hearts displayed an extraordinary resistance to the very idea that such a thing was possible. This adds mountains of credibility to their later witness. It is one thing to convince someone who desperately wants to believe. It's another thing to win over a skeptic.

On the road to Emmaus, Jesus called them "slow of heart to believe," yet over the next forty days they came to believe so completely that Jesus lived, they all willingly died rather than deny it.

The late Charles Colson, the Watergate co-conspirator who was radically saved in prison and went on to become one of the great Christian minds of the last half of the twentieth century, had this very reality in mind when he wrote:

> In my Watergate experience I saw the inability of men—powerful, highly motivated professionals—to hold together a conspiracy based on a lie...The actual cover-up lasted less than a month. Yet Christ's powerless followers maintained to their grim deaths by execution that they had in fact seen Jesus Christ raised from the dead. There was no conspiracy, no passover plot. Men and women do not give up their comfort—and certainly not their lives—for what they know to be a lie.[2]

When they finally believed, they truly believed.

† † † † †

The famous "Roman Road" to salvation begins at Romans 3:23 with, "For all have sinned and come short of the glory of God." It then winds through Romans 6:23, where a signpost informs the traveler that "the wages of sin is death, but the gift of God is eternal life through Jesus Christ our Lord." It then takes us directly to Calvary and to a battered, bleeding sin offering where love is on display. "But God demonstrates His own love toward us, in that while we were yet sinners, Christ died for us," says Romans 5:8.

That blessed highway to heaven ends at Romans 10:9. There even the vilest sinner discovers, "that if you confess with your mouth Jesus is Lord, *and believe in your heart that God has raised Him from the dead*, you will be saved" (emphasis added).

Notice please that here in the heart of Paul's master treatise on New Covenant theology, he declares belief in Jesus's resurrection to be one of the twin pillars of a profession of saving faith. Paul understood what many today have forgotten or never knew: without the Resurrection, there is no gospel. No Christianity. No church. No hope. No transcendent meaning to be found in life or living.

The Resurrection distinguishes our vital, world-transforming faith from mere religion and self-help sects. Without a literal, physical resurrection of Jesus of Nazareth from the dead, our faith is just another empty creed among the world's thousands of cults. Jesus Christ declared Himself to be the Way, the Truth, and the Life. Without His resurrection on the third day, we may as well stand Jesus on a platform beside Buddha, Muhammad, Krishna, and all the rest, a sorry spectacle over which the angels of heaven would hang their heads in solemn sadness and weep for eternity.

As Paul declares in the fifteenth chapter of 1 Corinthians, if Christ is not risen:

- Our preaching is empty (v. 14)

- Our faith is in vain (v. 17)

- We are still in our sins (v. 17)

- Those who have fallen asleep in Christ have perished (v. 18)

- We are of all men most miserable (v. 19)

No, you cannot remove the reality of the Resurrection and have anything left but a pile of lifeless platitudes. Denying Christ's complete victory over death renders the Bible little more than the world's oldest self-help book. To remove the ever-living Christ from the gospel message is to tear the heart out of the faith.

Is it any wonder then that the reality of the Resurrection is so frequently the focal point of Satan's attacks? The enemy of mankind detests the doctrine of the Resurrection more than any other. Why wouldn't he? His losing battle to retain death's hold on Jesus's soul was his Waterloo. His defeat in that struggle of the ages not only kicked open the door of hope for all of humanity, it also sealed his eternal doom.

Along these lines Albert Mohler, president of the Southern Baptist Theological Seminary, has written:

> The resurrection of Jesus Christ has been under persistent attacks since the Apostolic age. Why? Because it is the central confirmation of Jesus's identity as the incarnate Son of God, and the ultimate sign of Christ's completed work of atonement, redemption, reconciliation,

and salvation. Those who oppose Christ, whether first century religious leaders or twentieth century secularists, recognize the Resurrection as the vindication of Christ against His enemies.[3]

Yes, Satan has made sure that skeptics, deniers, and self-styled debunkers have abounded through the centuries.

As we have seen, within a few hours of Jesus's escape from that stony prison, the truth of the Resurrection was slandered with a bought-and-paid-for lie. The religious leaders parted with an enormous sum of money to acquire the false witness of the Roman guards. Matthew, writing roughly twenty-five years after the extraordinary events of this weekend, indicated that this lie—that Jesus's disciples had stolen His body in the night—remained "commonly reported among the Jews to this day" (Matt. 28:15).

Wherever the devil has been unable to assail the church's confidence in the Resurrection with attacks from the outside, he has endeavored to weaken and dilute it from within. There were the Docetic and Gnostic heresies in the early centuries of Christian history. Their counterparts in our time are the efforts by liberal theologians to remake the Christian faith in modern man's image.

Professor James Bissett Pratt, in his work, *The Psychology of Religious Belief* of 1908, predicted, "It [the Bible] has lost all hold on the leaders of thought and is certainly destined before very many years to become one of the curiosities of the past."[4] Reverend Harry Fosdick's theories led him to proclaim, "Of course I do not believe in the Virgin Birth, or in that old fashioned substitutionary doctrine of the atonement; and I do not know any intelligent Christian minister who does."[5] Another one of my favorite quotes comes from Theodore Parker, "As liberals in religion why should we commemorate the death of Jesus?...Jesus is not the center of our religion...Why do we not commemorate the life of Emerson or of Socrates or of Immanuel Kant?"[6]

The father of all these "enlightened ones" in the twentieth century was the late Paul Tillich, a liberal theologian and existential philosopher of enormous influence. Tillich was a rationalist who viewed the miracles of the Bible as symbolic myths rather than actual events. For Tillich, the Bible's accounts concerning the Cross, the Resurrection, and the Ascension are all symbolic and not to be taken literally—the miracle of the Resurrection least of all.

These modern "deep thinkers," with their gifts for intellectualizing simple truths into absurdities, put me in mind of a great passage from one of Spurgeon's sermons. He surely had Tillich's intellectual forefathers in mind when he preached:

> The word which the common people heard gladly is not fine enough for cultured sages, and so they must needs surround it with a mist of human thought and speculation...men want novelties; they cannot endure that the trumpet should give forth the same certain sound, they crave some fresh fantasia every day. "*The gospel with variations*" is the music for them. Intellect is progressive, they say; they must, therefore, march ahead of their forefathers. Incarnate Deity, a holy life, an atoning death, and a literal resurrection—having heard these things now for nearly nineteen centuries they are just a little stale, and the cultivated mind hungers for a change from the old fashioned manna.[7]

No, there is nothing new about the skeptics' efforts or arguments against a literal resurrection. They have ever and always assailed the great wall of this doctrinal truth and the historical reality behind it. They invariably fail. They cannot break the truth. They can only break themselves upon it. Light dispels darkness, and the darkness cannot overcome it.

Our definition of God's truth does not even get us beyond the shore, much less let us swim in the infinite ocean of the vastness of God. He is incomprehensible. He is inconceivable. He cannot be measured. His ability cannot be calculated. He is the infinite God, and with Him all things are possible.

Job, who wrote the oldest book in your Bible, had a measure of understanding about the infinite power of God. Job 26:7 says, "He stretches out the north over empty space, He hangs the earth upon nothing."

Astronomers tell us that in the northernmost part of the intergalactic nebulae, above the constellation Orion, sixteen trillion, six hundred forty billion miles in diameter, is a gaping black hole. Over ninety Milky Way galaxies could fit into the opening of that one hole in the vastness of space. The psalmist said, "Is Mount Zion, on the sides of the north, the city of the great King" (Ps. 48:2). Our God fills all in all.

The notion that God is omnipotent, omniscient, and omnipresent has fallen out of favor in our enlightened age. In the 1960s, so-called educated men sat in their chairs in their ivory towers of academia, stroked their goatees, encircled their brows with a wreath of smoke from their pipes, and declared with solemnity and certainty that God was dead.

I have a few questions. If God is dead, who was His assassin? Where is the cemetery plot that contains His remains, and where is the tombstone upon which is etched His name? If God is dead, how many men would be strong enough to carry His coffin to its final resting place? Where is the funeral home that handled His arrangements? And if God is dead, why wasn't I notified? I'm a member of His family!

Psalm 14:1 says, "The fool has said in his heart, 'There is no God.'" God cannot die by assassination, by accident, or by the proclamation of fools. He will never die—He is eternal—nor will He ever grow weary. He will outlast all the deniers and the skeptics.

He will not cease to exist because of backslidden church boards and lazy and lustful pulpiteers. He will not be affected by the leaven of the modern Pharisees, who pile on their religious rules and rudiments, nor will He be diminished by the modern Sadducees with their weighty volumes declaring He does not exist.

How big is your God? He'll provide for you as He did for Peter when He told him he would catch a fish with a coin in its mouth. He'll heal you today just as He healed blind Bartimaeus begging by the roadside. He'll deliver you today, the same way He set the man in Gadara free who was possessed by a legion of demon spirits. He is the same yesterday, today, and forever!

Since the declaration that God is dead didn't gain a lot of traction, the erudite and elite changed course and said, "If God is not dead, where did He come from?" Their purpose, of course, was not to engage in a legitimate discussion, but to ensnare believers just as the Pharisees sought to trap Jesus into saying something about which they could accuse Him to the authorities. The skeptics' logic went like this: if God had a beginning, then we can argue that He also has an ending.

I have more good news for you—God didn't come from anywhere. He always has been, from eternity past, when there was nowhere to come from. Job said He hung the earth upon nothing.

God came from nowhere, because there was nowhere to come from—then He reached out into nothing, since there was nothing to reach for. Then He grabbed something that wasn't there, since there was nothing to grab, and pulled it out of nowhere and hung it on nothing. And He pointed His finger at it and told it to stay where He put it. And nobody disagreed with Him, because there was nobody there besides Him. And He folded His arms and said, "It is good."

Louis L'Amour, the prolific western writer, said this: "There will come a time when you believe everything is finished. Yet that will be the beginning."[8] Jesus cried from the cross, "It is finished." What He meant was the battle had been won and victory was assured—but even though one story had come to an end, the next one was about to begin.

God never brings us to a consummation without an initiation. He is not Alpha and Omega as though He is on a continuous line. Nor is He just a circle that has no beginning or end. He is infinite. The scientific symbol for infinity is a figure that looks like the number eight on its side. It is a never-ending double loop that never stops.

Every loop gives Him propulsion into the next curve, which creates velocity for the next loop. He creates His own energy. He needs nothing to get going or to continue. He is inexhaustible. Your need does not diminish His supply but prompts His provision, and when He has met your need, He has more than before you had a need. What a great God we serve! In one way, to affirm that God and His truth need to be defended from man's denials is like saying that an elephant needs to be defended from an ant. However, for those who have a genuine interest in knowing the truth, many wonderful books have been devoted to demonstrating the evidences and proofs of the Resurrection. There are a number of works of outstanding scholarship that demolish the skeptics' arguments and make a persuasive case for the historical resurrection of the founder of the Christian faith. Thus I will not devote space here to restating those arguments.

All of these powerful defenses and presentations of "convincing proofs," as Luke called them, are wonderful. I thank God for them. Eventually, however, all encounters with God come down not to reason but to faith. There is nothing wrong with reason. Indeed, nothing on earth is more rational than placing one's life in the hands of a loving Father God. But God has, by design, left just enough of our questions unanswered that faith will always be necessary for us to make the leap into His waiting arms. Eventually everyone who experiences the regenerative miracle of the new birth must come to a place in which they say, with Job, "I know that my redeemer liveth" (Job 19:25, KJV).

That place, located at the terminus of salvation's Roman Road, is a place of faith, not facts. You arrive through spirit conviction, not mind persuasion.

The reluctant, fearful, doubting disciples came to that place. So has every lost and wandering soul who ever found mercy and healing at the foot of Calvary. That journey doesn't end at the cross, however. It invariably takes each of us down that cruel hill to a nearby garden where a tomb stands empty. There you and I, and every person ever given an opportunity to hear the gospel message, have a decision to make.

You see, the angel didn't roll that stone away so Jesus could get out. He removed it so we could look in and, having seen that it is empty, choose.

One of God's greatest gifts to mankind is that of free will. Deuteronomy 30:19 reminds us that He sets before us life and death, and then, in His infinite wisdom, He admonishes us to choose life. As for me, my decision is made. I confidently say that He lives!

Chapter 8

LIVING in RESURRECTION POWER

Since all power on Earth is lodged in Christ's hands,
He can also clothe any and all of His servants with
a sacred might... You are very feeble, and you know
it, but there is no reason why you should not be
strong in Him. If you look to the strong for strength,
He can endue you with power from on high.[1]

> CHARLES SPURGEON
> (1834–1892)

ETER BOLTED THE door as a few of the women hung coverings over the window openings to conceal the lamplight burning within. It was late at night on what will one day come to be known as the first Easter. Twenty or thirty of Jesus's core disciples and family had reassembled to discuss the wild reports some members of the group had been bringing—accounts of angelic visitations and encounters with their recently executed leader. Of the eleven living disciples, only Thomas was absent.

They were sleep deprived and spent, both physically and emotionally. Most remained in mortal dread of being arrested just as Jesus had been two days ago. Even so, those among them who believed they'd seen something extraordinary were clearly exhilarated. Most of them, however, remained highly skeptical of the strange reports they'd been hearing. John was an exception. He returned from an early morning investigative visit to the tomb with Peter exhibiting a strange calm—one he had carried throughout the day. Initially, Peter returned from the tomb convinced the body had been stolen. But now even he, like the women and the two men just back from Emmaus, was claiming to have personally seen the Master alive.

Four or five clusters of hushed conversation were simultaneously underway in the large room when suddenly a newcomer stood in their midst. "Peace be with you," they heard Him say. How well they knew that voice. How much they missed that face. It is He. It is true! He lives!

Can you imagine it? If there were any place your Bible could have exaggerated, it would've been right here. Instead, it simply states, "The disciples were then *glad* when they saw the Lord" (John 20:20, emphasis added). No motion, no emotion, no commotion. Friend, I happen to believe they were more than *glad* when they saw the Lord! Now that they knew He had risen from the dead and was alive, there was absolutely nothing they couldn't do, for with God nothing—or *no thing*—is impossible. The possibilities were endless, their hope was renewed, and the disciples certainly must have been elated to see the Lord.

Over the next forty days the eleven remaining disciples enjoyed periodic encounters and seasons of fellowship with the risen Christ. There was a breakfast of fresh roasted fish by the Sea of Galilee and a mountaintop meeting in which He revealed their long-term marching orders. They were going to be sent to "all nations" where they would baptize "in the name of the Father and of the Son and of the Holy Spirit" and teach them to observe all the things He commanded them. (See Matthew

28:19–20.) Then, roughly ten days prior to the Jerusalem Feast of Weeks, or Pentecost, He gave them another very specific set of instructions:

> Do not depart from Jerusalem, but wait for the promise of the Father, of which you have heard from Me. For John baptized with water, but you shall be baptized with the Holy Spirit not many days from now.
>
> —ACTS 1:4–5

He previously had told them their assignment was to "go." Now they learned that before they could go, they must "wait." Wait for what? The Father had promised something. A baptism, but one unlike the water baptism they received from John. That baptism immersed them and covered them outwardly. They did not know it yet, but this coming baptism would both cover and fill.

After delivering this directive, Jesus led them down that familiar road to Bethany—a Sabbath day's walk—one last time. There they assembled on a hillside outside of the village. After answering a final question about the status of national Israel, Jesus then delivered the last insight they would ever hear Him utter in the flesh. Final words are important words. This message represented the "P.S." on the love letter that was His life. It was the exclamatory punctuation mark on everything He had poured into them through three-and-a-half years of mentoring, modeling, and discipling. Just before being caught up and disappearing into the clouds, He spoke of this promised baptism once more:

> But you shall receive power when the Holy Spirit comes upon you. And you shall be My witnesses in Jerusalem, and in all Judea and Samaria, and to the ends of the earth.
>
> —ACTS 1:8

Power! Heavenly power. This is what they lacked. This and this alone enables mere mortals to carry out audacious orders to go into all the world and conquer it with love. Only power produces nation shakers and culture lifters. Nothing else transforms cowards and doubters into bold witnesses who love not their lives even unto death.

What if this "promise of the Father" were true? What would happen if redeemed men and women could actually be endued with power from on high? Could it be that simple fishermen and humble maidservants might really find themselves filled with the very same power that raised Jesus from the dead?

After a period of worshipping the Savior who had just been received into heaven before their astonished eyes, the men headed back to Jerusalem to learn the answer to that question. The Master had said to wait, and that was precisely what they intended to do.

God Himself instituted the observance of Pentecost, or the Feast of Weeks, through Moses. It stood as one of three major "pilgrimage feasts" in Israel and occurred precisely fifty days after the Festival of Firstfruits in which the high priest lifted an *omer* of barley flour in a wave offering to the Lord. Until the Roman armies destroyed the Jerusalem temple in AD 70, Jews throughout the Roman world traveled to Jerusalem three times a year to sacrifice and celebrate these feasts of pilgrimage—the Passover and Pentecost in the spring, Tabernacles in the fall.

Each feast pointed back to a major event surrounding the Exodus from Egypt and the sojourn to the land of promise. For example, the Passover feast commemorated the event centuries earlier in Egypt when the spirit of death passed over the children of Israel on the night before their great deliverance from bondage. On that night, they were delivered by painting their doorposts with the blood of an unblemished lamb. That event also foreshadowed the coming day when all humanity would be offered deliverance from slavery to sin and eternal death through the blood of Jesus, the spotless Lamb of God. As for Pentecost, it pointed back to God giving the law to Moses on Mount Sinai fifty days after the Exodus from Egypt.

The Day of Pentecost found the disciples with more than one hundred other Jesus followers praying, singing, and fellowshipping in a large house in central Jerusalem. They were following Jesus's explicit instructions to wait in the city until "the promise of the Father" came. That day their waiting ended:

> When the day of Pentecost had come, they were all together in one place. Suddenly a sound like a mighty rushing wind came from heaven, and it filled the whole house where they were sitting. There appeared to them tongues as of fire, being distributed and resting on each of them, and they were all filled with the Holy Spirit and began to speak in other tongues, as the Spirit enabled them to speak.
>
> —ACTS 2:1–4

For the eleven original disciples of Jesus and one hundred and nine other men and women assembled in that house on Pentecost Sunday, the mighty outpouring of the Holy Ghost was a watershed moment. It created an indelible line on the calendar of their lives and on the timeline of human history—a game changer for the ages.

Discrete and diverse units of humanity became unified. Individuals became amalgamated into something that none of them were on their own. A whole was born that was far greater than the sum of the individual parts. A new social order was welded and melded together. And God meant for this new order to spread like wildfire. This divine passport blew them across all barriers of race and religion, and most of all, above mediocrity. They were no longer spectators of Jesus or merely fans of the message, but the church had received the undeniable infusion and infilling of the Spirit just as Jesus had promised!

Before that day, the disciples were fearful and faint hearted, cowering in locked rooms and flinching at every knock at the door. From that day forward, a fierce boldness characterized their lives and ministries. They proclaimed Jesus in public squares and synagogues and were impervious to threats of arrest, beatings, or even death. They carried no dread of the disapproval of man.

Before that baptism from heaven, they struggled to comprehend the Scriptures. After their fiery immersion, the scales fell from their eyes. They instantly saw how the entire Old Testament pointed to Jesus. What had previously been shrouded in mystery suddenly became utterly clear. Peter demonstrated this by immediately walking outside and preaching a spontaneous sermon that cited and expounded upon numerous Old Testament passages.

This was the "Helper" Jesus had promised in one of His final talks with His disciples, the One who would lead them into all truth and show them things to come. (See John 16:13.) Those tongues as of flame that rested on each of them supernaturally branded these men and women with the fire of God Himself. The effects were extraordinary, visible, and audible. As Luke recounts:

> Now dwelling in Jerusalem were Jews, devout men, from every nation under heaven. When this sound occurred, the crowd came together and were confounded, because each man heard them speaking in his own language. They were all amazed and marveled, saying to each other,

> "Are not all these who are speaking Galileans? How is it
> that we hear, each in our own native language?"
> —ACTS 2:5–8

This was a double-miracle sign to a lost world. The Spirit-baptized believers were speaking languages they did not know. And each hearer in the diverse, multinational crowd was hearing them in his or her native tongue.

Of course, whenever the power and purity of God are on public display, scoffers, skeptics, and dismissers invariably have an opinion to share. This day was no exception. Luke reports, "Others mocking said, 'These men are full of new wine'" (Acts 2:13).

Peter and the other disciples—all freshly infused with a power they had never before carried—took their stand on a rooftop balcony of the house. Peter spoke for the group and addressed the scoffers first.

> But Peter, standing up with the eleven, lifted up his voice
> and said to them, "Men of Judea and all you who dwell
> in Jerusalem, let this be known to you, and listen to my
> words. For these are not drunk, as you suppose, since it is
> the third hour of the day. But this is what was spoken by
> the prophet Joel."
> —ACTS 2:14–16

No, these men were not drunk, but they were "under the influence" of a behavior-altering "Spirit." It is no coincidence that inebriation was the topic on this occasion, in that there are some interesting parallels between that and the influence of the Holy Spirit on a believer. Indeed, years later Paul would link the two, writing, "And be not drunk with wine, wherein is excess; but be filled with the Spirit" (Eph. 5:18, KJV). As a brief aside, allow me to share eight characteristics of drunkenness in the natural that actually have a holy parallel to those who are truly filled with Holy Ghost power. Here is what happens when you are under the influence of His power.

1. You see others differently. Back in the 1970s there was a country music song titled, "Don't the Girls All Get Prettier at Closing Time?" Binge-drinking frat boys everywhere use the term "beer goggles" to refer to the way intoxication tends to recalibrate their ability to assess attractiveness. In a similar way, when you're under the influence of the Holy Spirit, everyone looks good. You're less critical. It's easier to walk in love toward others. As 1 Corinthians informs us, love "bears all things, believes all things, hopes all things, and endures all things" (1 Cor. 13:7).

2. You hear voices and see things. Chronic alcoholics routinely end up having hallucinations. The Spirit-baptized believer hears that still, small voice and sees what others cannot see. Paul said, "while we do not look at the things which are seen, but at the things which are not seen. For the things which are seen are temporal, but the things which are not seen are eternal" (2 Cor. 4:18). Mere mortals cannot "look" at something that is "not seen," but those under the Spirit's influence can and do.

3. You can't help but sing. The tipsy individual belting out a song is not an uncommon sight among those who have lost their inhibitions due to the intake of "liquid confidence." In a similar way, those overflowing with the Spirit of God can't help but sing either, and often in the most unlikely places and under unfavorable circumstances. Paul and Silas sang at midnight while shackled in a filthy dungeon. When God's anointing fell upon him, the psalmist David composed soaring songs of praise in the midst of his darkest trials. Paul immediately followed his instructions to be filled with the Spirit rather than drunk with wine with this advice: "Speak to one another in psalms, hymns, and spiritual songs, singing and making melody in your heart to the Lord" (Eph. 5:19).

4. You emanate a distinctive odor. Most people can immediately recognize someone who has been drinking by the smell that accompanies them, by the scent of alcohol on their breath. The Spirit-baptized individual carries a fragrance as well. In the Old Testament, the oil of anointing was infused with myrrh and spices to give it a sweet fragrance. The anointing of the Holy Spirit has the same effect. Paul said, "For we are to God a sweet fragrance of Christ among those who are saved and among those who perish" (2 Cor. 2:15). It is an aroma that attracts the favor of God!

5. You strip off your clothes. I know this is scandalous, but it surely comes as no surprise to you that when someone is drinking to the point that their inhibitions have escaped them, they are likely to shed their clothes. In my decades of being around Spirit-filled believers, I have noted that they too are prone to making a wardrobe change. It's the one described in Isaiah 61:3: "to preserve those who mourn in Zion, to give to them beauty for ashes, the oil of joy for mourning, the garment of praise for the spirit of heaviness." Those who drink deeply of the well of God's presence just cannot seem to keep those old rags of despair, gloom, or self-pity on. They're constantly stripping them off and donning shining garments of hope, gratitude, and praise instead. They know they're going to the wedding feast of a King soon, and they want to be dressed appropriately.

6. You lose your mind. Slurred speech, incoherent ramblings, and fuzzy logic are all hallmarks of inebriation. On the Day of Pentecost, the outpouring of the Holy Spirit had a profound effect on both the speech and the thinking of the new Spirit-filled believers. They not only spoke with other tongues as the Spirit gave them utterance, they also stopped depending on the flawed logic and perverted wisdom of fallen man. Paul had this effect in mind when he told the church in Corinth:

> Brothers, when I came to you, I did not come with superiority of speech or wisdom, declaring to you the testimony of God...My speech and my preaching was not with enticing words of man's wisdom, but in demonstration of the Spirit and of power, so that your faith should not stand in the wisdom of men, but in the power of God.
>
> —1 CORINTHIANS 2:1, 4–5

7. You look for a fight. The belligerent, combative drunk is so common it has become a cliché. When some people drink they tend to be easily offended and excessively brave. Bars and clubs remain the most common settings for fights for a very good reason. The believer freshly filled with the Spirit is easily offended by the works of Satan in the lives of others and will fearlessly assault the gates of hell to see them freed. The difference is that a fully armed and armored believer is guaranteed victory. Jesus said, "Look, I give you authority to trample on serpents and scorpions, and over all the power of the enemy. And nothing shall by any means hurt you" (Luke 10:19). And Paul said, "the weapons of our warfare are not carnal, but mighty through God to the pulling down of strongholds" (2 Cor. 10:4).

8. You become generous. I had an uncle named Willie who was an alcoholic for thirty years before being gloriously saved and transformed by the power of Jesus Christ. I remember one particular occasion when I was a boy. He was over at our house and had that funny smell on his breath. He looked at me, waved his hand around the room, and slurred, "Do you like this house? You can have it. I'll give it to you!" The problem was that the house wasn't his to give. The fact is, some people get remarkably generous when they are under the influence of alcohol. In a similar way, believers become a lot less attached to their "stuff" when under the influence of the Holy Spirit. Indeed, before Luke concludes the second chapter of Acts, he will report, "All who believed were together and had all things in common. They sold their property and goods and distributed them to all, according to their need" (vv. 44–45).

Yes, it is impossible to overstate the significance of the Holy Spirit's outpouring upon the church of Jesus Christ collectively or the difference His power makes in the life of an individual. The disciples walked out of that room changed from the inside out.

Let's pick up Peter's sermon where we left off. It merits attention because, as noted previously, this is the very first sermon ever preached by a Holy Spirit–baptized man. He informs his listeners that a key Old Testament prophecy has just been fulfilled right before their eyes and ears. He says, "But this is what was spoken by the prophet Joel…" Then he quotes Joel at length:

> "In the last days it shall be," says God, "that I will pour out My Spirit on all flesh; your sons and your daughters shall prophesy, your young men shall see visions, and your old men shall dream dreams. Even on My menservants and maidservants I will pour out My Spirit in those days; and they shall prophesy."
>
> —ACTS 2:17–18

Allow me to interrupt Peter's quoting of Joel here to point out the mention in this prophecy of sons *and* daughters, young *and* old, menservants *and* maidservants. The Word of God is making it clear beyond any doubt that this outpouring of God's Spirit is for everyone, regardless of sex, age, class, or social standing. God is no respecter of persons. There will be no distinctions or divisions. The baptism in this Holy Spirit is for "whosoever will" receive. Peter's recitation of Joel's prophecy continues:

> "And I will show wonders in heaven above and signs on the earth below: blood, and fire, and vapor of smoke. The sun shall be turned into darkness, and the moon into blood, before that great and glorious day of the Lord comes. And whoever calls on the name of the Lord shall be saved."
>
> —ACTS 2:19–21

Please allow me to pause Peter's sermon once more and direct your attention to another aspect of Joel's prophecy. Here Joel speaks of wonders in the heavens and signs on the earth. He speaks of the sun being darkened (a total solar eclipse) and a turning of "the moon into blood" (a total lunar eclipse).

In 2015 and in several years preceding, millions of books were sold and countless conferences were sold out by Bible teachers pointing to a series of four total lunar eclipses that coincided with four key festivals on the Jewish calendar. The "red blood moon" tetrad had much of the evangelical world buzzing with expectation of some sort of end-time event. Indeed some Bible prophecy specialists went as far as to predict the return of Jesus Christ on the day of the final of these four blood moons in September of 2015.

Clearly, those predictions proved erroneous. The fact is, I did my best throughout those months to point out to whomever would listen that this series of lunar eclipses could not possibly be the one that signals Joel's "great and glorious day of the Lord."

I reminded my congregation and the audience of my international television broadcast that the "glorious day of the Lord"—His return to rule and reign on this earth—transpires *after* a seven-year period of great and dreadful tribulation.

Furthermore, that tribulation period only begins after the Rapture of the church. In other words, when the meaningful "blood moon" mentioned in Joel appears, the church will not be here to witness it! This is good news for every child of God.

In any event, Peter completes his impromptu message, and three thousand souls are saved right on the spot. This is what the anointing of God's Holy Spirit does when it covers and fills a frail and fallible child of God. It turns him or her into a conduit of God's power in the earth. I like to remind people that Peter prayed for ten days, preached for ten minutes, and three thousand were saved. Many preachers today pray for ten minutes, preach for what feels like ten days, and nothing happens.

That Day of Pentecost was a good day for you and me. It means Jesus sent the Helper, just as He'd promised. The question is, are we availing ourselves of His amazing help?

† † † † †

What does the great outpouring of the Holy Spirit on the Day of Pentecost have to do with an exploration of Jesus's resurrection? I will defer to the Apostle Paul in addressing that question. In Romans 8:11 he wrote:

> But if the Spirit of Him who raised Jesus from the dead lives in you, He who raised Christ from the dead will also give life to your mortal bodies through His Spirit that lives in you.

The implications of this little verse are stunning. Contemplate them for a moment. Holy Spirit power raised Jesus from the dead. That same Holy Spirit can live in you. If He does, that *same* power resides within you.

In John 11:24, Martha expressed her confidence that Lazarus would, at the last day, rise again. She didn't realize that Jesus had the power to raise him up right then. There is a corollary for you and me. Yes, if I die before the catching away of the church, the same power that raised Christ from the dead will indeed give life to my mortal body. I will attain to the resurrection of the dead and receive my glorified spirit body. But I don't have to wait for that day. I have been filled with the Holy Ghost, and His resurrection power is available to me now!

In other words, the Holy Spirit is the key to living in resurrection power! It is a lifestyle. It is a way of being and moving and operating in this fallen world. Paul surely had this in mind when he said he counted all things as loss that he might gain a far greater prize, that is, "to know Him, and the power of His resurrection" (Phil. 3:10).

This is what the church is missing today! The power of Pentecost. Resurrection power. We see a powerless, Pentecostless version of our faith on display on every corner. Is it any wonder we often see more perversion than power? More playboys than prophets? More compromise than conviction?

Oh, how we need the One who condescends to indwell mortals, to fill us full of Himself. But let us first count the cost. Though Pentecost meant power to the disciples, it was also prison to them. Pentecost meant enduement, but it also meant banishment from organized religion. Pentecost meant favor with God but invited the hatred of men. Pentecost brought great miracles, but it also brought mighty obstacles.

Many who claim they have experienced the baptism of the Holy Ghost are more dead than alive, more off than on, more wrong than right. Some are more Spirit-frilled than Spirit-filled. We have become so accustomed to dwelling on the outer fringes of His presence that we have forgotten the inner essence of His power. Our lack of fruit condemns our prayerless, powerless, passionless Christianity.

We have a shout in the sanctuary but no clout in the Spirit.

We claim authority but take no meaningful ground. We write songs of victory over evil more suitable for the playground than the battleground. We have become proficient in the dialect of men but devoid of the voice of heaven.

We need another drenching downpour of Pentecostal power. It is the same power that raised Jesus from the dead. And you can live in resurrection power today and every day!

PART IV:

MONDAY AND BEYOND

Chapter 9

OVER the HORIZON

*Our Lord has written the promise of resurrection
not in books alone, but in every leaf in springtime.*[1]

> ᐳ MARTIN LUTHER
> (1483–1546)

U NDER A STEEL-GRAY sky, the frigid streets of Moscow
are lined with shivering people and grim-faced military personnel wearing black armbands trimmed with
red. Here on November 15, 1982, Ronald Reagan's vice president,
future US president George H. W. Bush, stands with other dig-
nitaries near a massive black casket. At the height of the Cold
War, Soviet Premier Leonid Brezhnev is dead, and Bush is here
to represent his nation at the funeral. Years later, he will reveal
having witnessed something at the close of this service that
both stunned and moved him.

The vice president watches a long stream of Soviet bureau-
crats and generals file by the casket to pay their final respects
to the man who had been the leader of the world's largest, most
powerful, and possibly most brutal totalitarian regime. The late
Mao's China is a contender for that last distinction.

The Soviet empire was born in 1917 on Marxist-Communist principles that outlawed all forms of religion other than worship of the state. By definition and under threat of punishment, good Soviet men and women were science-centered materialists: people who believe that the material world is all that exists. All religion was outlawed, with Christianity considered the most dangerous "superstition" of all. It also proved the most difficult to eradicate. The evil empire filled its infamous "archipelago" of gulags, or concentration camps, with stubborn Christians.

After the last of the mourners files past Brezhnev's casket, his seventy-four-year-old widow, Viktoria, rises to say her final good-bye. She stands silently beside the body of her late husband for several moments, her face unseen behind a long black mourner's veil. Then she nods to the military pallbearers standing nearby, signaling her readiness for them to lower the casket lid.

Then, just as the soldiers begin to do so, the grieving widow does something that draws an astonished gasp from every witness with a line of sight to the casket. Quickly reaching into the coffin, she makes the sign of the cross over her dead husband's chest.

This woman was born into the atheistic Soviet system. She spent her entire adult life in a culture that viewed Christianity as a mental disorder so dangerous and demented that it justified the brutal institutionalization of those who professed it. Yet none of that could extinguish a flickering flame of hope in her soul that this life is not all there is. One journalist described her courageous and desperate act in these terms:

> There in the citadel of secular, atheistic power, the wife of the man who had run it all hoped that her husband was wrong. She hoped that there was another life, and that that life was best represented by Jesus who died on the

cross, and that the same Jesus might yet have mercy on her husband.[2]

As the world-weary preacher in Ecclesiastes observed, God has set eternity in the human heart. It is simply unnatural for a man to believe that death is the end of his story. Yet some succeed.

The evolutionist and militant atheist Richard Dawkins is a heroic figure to the world's large and growing cadre of anti-Christian skeptics. Given the numerous testimonies of Jesus's empty tomb, Dawkins was once asked what he thought had happened to Jesus's body. He answered, "Presumably what happened to Jesus was what happens to all of us when we die. We decompose. Accounts of Jesus's resurrection and ascension are about as well-documented as Jack and the Beanstalk."[3]

Dr. Dawkins is, of course, wrong in every respect. He is also in for quite a surprise someday. Doubters and skeptics have always been with us. In fact, more than nineteen centuries ago the Apostle Paul felt compelled to write these words:

> Now if Christ is preached that He rose from the dead, how can some of you say that there is no resurrection of the dead?
> —1 Corinthians 15:12

As we have already seen, the entire fifteenth chapter of 1 Corinthians represents Paul's *tour de force* case for the reality of the resurrection of Jesus Christ. It is much more than that, however. Throughout the chapter Paul links Jesus's resurrection to yours and mine. He rightly states that if the dead can't be raised, then Jesus wasn't raised. And if Jesus was not raised, then the entire edifice of Christian belief collapses like a house of cards.

Jesus lives! Thanks be to God! And because He lives, we

have hope beyond the scope of human limitation. You can have hope that dead things in your life can be revived! Perhaps there was a dream that you once held dear and now it seems as though it's completely out of reach. When do you dream? In the dark. When did Jesus emerge from the tomb? In the dark. Friend, I want to proclaim to you that it's time to dream again! Resurrection power is available to you in any area of your life, even when circumstances look bleak and beyond your control!

No matter who you are, regardless of what your present standing is with God—whether you are a spotless saint or the vilest, God-despising sinner—there is a personal resurrection in your future. The only open question is, "Which one?" You see, God has at least two additional resurrections still to come on His agenda of the ages.

The first of these is the resurrection of the millions upon millions of righteous, born-again saints who have died since Jesus emptied out the Paradise side of Sheol at His resurrection. These spirits of the righteous dead have been in heaven since dying, but at this resurrection they will receive new, glorified spiritual bodies like the one with which Jesus came forth from His tomb. This represents the next event on God's prophetic calendar, and it centers upon Jesus, the Bridegroom, calling forth His bride for the great wedding feast.

Of course, if you are assembling all the saints on the earth for a wedding feast, you have to do *something* with the believers who happen to still be alive the moment that trumpet blast gives the signal for the righteous dead to rise. Paul described that moment in these words to the church at Thessalonica:

> For the Lord Himself will descend from heaven with a shout, with the voice of the archangel, and with the trumpet call of God. And the dead in Christ will rise first. Then we who are alive and remain shall be caught

up together with them in the clouds to meet the Lord in the air. And so we shall be forever with the Lord.

—1 THESSALONIANS 4:16–17

This event is commonly called "the Rapture" of the church. What many do not understand is that the catching away of the living saints in this extraordinary event is a by-product of the "main event," that is, the first resurrection. Yes, there is a specific *order* in God's plan for resurrecting deceased humanity. Paul references this order in his resurrection treatise:

For as in Adam all die, even so in Christ shall all be made alive. *But every man in his own order:* Christ the first fruits; afterward, those who are Christ's at His coming.

—1 CORINTHIANS 15:22–23,

EMPHASIS ADDED

In God's order, the righteous go first. This resurrection of the saints is not, however, the final time the dead shall rise. Jesus once spoke of a "resurrection of judgment." (See John 5:28–29.) When does this resurrection of judgment take place?

According to the Book of Revelation, this will occur only after the thousand-year millennial reign of Jesus Christ upon the earth. Referring to the initial resurrection of the righteous, Revelation 20:5 specifically says, "The rest of the dead did not come to life until the thousand years were ended. This is the first resurrection." A few verses later John sees a vision of a "Great White Throne."

Then I saw a great white throne and Him who was seated on it. From His face the earth and the heavens fled away, and no place was found for them. And I saw the dead, small and great, standing before God. Books were opened. Then another book was opened, which is the Book of Life. The dead were judged according to their works as recorded in the books. The sea gave up the dead who were in it, and Death and Hades delivered up the dead who were in them. And they were judged, each one by his works.

—REVELATION 20:11–13

Here is the "resurrection of judgment" Jesus referenced. The fact remains, we will all rise at one time or the other, whether in the "resurrection of life" or the "resurrection of judgment."

Dear friend, you do not want to be a part of that second resurrection. Come with me. I am going in the first load out—whether by resurrection or by Rapture!

In considering the concept of eternity, I want you to be aware of two very important facts. First, everyone is going to live forever. It's in this lifetime where each person chooses that destination—either heaven or hell. I hope you've accepted Jesus Christ as your Lord and therefore are guaranteed a home in heaven with Him. Second, everyone is going to heaven. Yes, it's true! But allow me to finish this weighty statement: not everyone gets to stay. We will all appear before the Son of Man, and He will separate us. Those on His right He will welcome into His Father's kingdom, but those on His left will be banished to eternity in hell. (See Matthew 25:34–40.)

I plead with you, if you haven't made Jesus Christ the Lord of your life, do so right now. Simply repent of your sins and ask Him to come into your heart. God will honor your prayer, and I can assure you that it will be the best decision of your life.

✝ ✝ ✝ ✝ ✝

In the opening verses of his letter to the Romans, Paul states plainly that he writes to them "concerning His Son, Jesus Christ our Lord, who was born of the seed of David according to the flesh and declared to be the Son of God with power, according to the Spirit of holiness, by the resurrection from the dead" (Rom. 1:3–4).

Here we have the conundrum of the incarnation. The infinite God somehow subjected Himself to the limitations of human flesh. He "was born of the seed of David according to the flesh," indicating His humanity, but "declared to be the Son of God with power, according to the spirit of holiness, by the resurrection from the dead." Jesus Christ was the God-man. Not merely deity humanized. Not merely humanity deified. He was both and neither. At once, all God and all man. Our limited minds stumble and stagger to grasp this precisely because there is not another like Him in heaven or earth. Thankfully we don't need to understand God to worship and adore Him.

Please notice that, according to Paul, the act of resurrection "declared" Jesus to be who He claimed to be, that is, the only begotten Son of God. The Greek word Paul chose here is *horizo*, one that means "to establish the outermost boundary or limit." It obviously serves as the root source of our English word *horizon*. Paul uses the past tense version of this Greek verb and therefore proclaims, in a sense, that Jesus was "horizoned" by His resurrection from the dead. Perhaps there is more here than we have appreciated.

As a boy growing up amid the gently rolling hills and abundant trees of central Ohio, I never got a proper look at the horizon. Vistas never stretched more than a mile or two before being interrupted by a building, a hill, or a stand of trees. Only a trip to the ocean afforded me my first-ever glimpse of a true horizon—the edge of perception where sky meets sea.

For the ancients, the horizon was viewed to be the outermost boundary—the limit beyond which no one could pass. As voyagers ventured further and further from land, they realized there was more to the world than their senses could perceive from a fixed point. As a result, the wild postulations of brilliant dreamers who had dared suggest the world was not flat seemed less preposterous. In other words, the limits of human sight did not represent the limit of human existence. There was a new world waiting for man just beyond the horizon.

Death, of course, was the ultimate horizon. It marked the terminal limit of our human senses. No person could see beyond the veil of death. No one could perceive what lay behind that thick, black curtain. Death represented the last, impenetrable boundary for earthly men. For countless generations, no one escaped its unyielding grip. No person who entered that realm ever returned to report about its contours or its climate.

Yes, some cultures cultivated myths and legends of existence beyond the grave, but they possessed no tangible proof that such tales were true. Even Jesus's disciples instantly surrendered to despair upon seeing His lifeless body. They locked themselves away and trembled in fear to see Him who commanded wind and waves, demons and death itself, lying cold on a slab of stone. The Roman spear pierced more than Jesus's side that day. It killed their hope.

Hope lay cold and lifeless in the ground for two days. The Lord of Life had stepped beyond the horizon. Then Sunday morning came and with it a message to startled women bearing anointing oils. "Do not be afraid. For I know that you are looking for Jesus who was crucified. He is not here. For He has risen, as He said. Come, see the place where the Lord lay" (Matt. 28:5–6).

He is gone. Hope lives.

This is the message I have been commissioned to carry in my generation. To the best of my frail ability, yet empowered by the same enabling that raised Jesus Christ from the dead, I have endeavored to deliver this glorious truth. Because He lives, hope lives. No matter what you've done, no matter what your circumstances, no matter how dark your midnight, that same resurrection power is available to you right now. This is the gospel of Jesus Christ. If God is able to get Jesus out of the grave, He can deliver you from death in all of its profane and destructive manifestations.

You see, what the ancients thought was the end isn't really an end at all—just as the horizon is not the edge of the world, and death is no longer the necessary end for you and me. In traveling to the realm of death, Jesus Christ, the God-Man, sailed beyond the horizon. In returning with the keys of death and hell in His possession, He removed the constraints of man's perception, knowledge, and understanding. Now, in Him, the sons and daughters of Adam could go beyond the limits that had held them in spiritual paralysis since the Garden of Eden.

The Apostle Paul got a peek beyond the horizon. Once caught up into "the third heaven," he was shown things few if any living men had glimpsed. Fortunately, he did not keep the mysteries to which he was uniquely privy to himself. He wrote to friends like you and me, saying:

> Listen, I tell you a mystery: We shall not all sleep, but we shall all be changed. In a moment, in the twinkling of an eye, at the last trumpet, for the trumpet will sound, the dead will be raised incorruptible, and we shall be changed. For this corruptible will put on incorruption, and this mortal will put on immortality. When this corruptible will have put on incorruption, and this mortal will have put on immortality, then the saying that is written shall come to pass: "Death is swallowed up in victory."
>
> "O death, where is your sting? O grave, where is your victory?"
>
> —1 CORINTHIANS 15:51–55

I know the answer to Paul's final two questions. Death's sting has been rendered impotent by the overpowering impact of the Resurrection. The grave's victory has been turned into total defeat as the Prince of Life arose victorious over all its power on Resurrection Morning. The greatest of our Almighty God's displays of omnipotence has provided the centerpiece of our faith. As the angels announced to the women who tarried at the tomb, "He is not here. For He has risen, as He said" (Matt. 28:6).

He is *gone* from there but has ascended to heaven. He is absent from the tomb, but present in the hearts of all who have accepted Him as Savior. He is no longer shrouded in grave clothes and hidden behind a stone, but displayed in glory and majesty for a skeptical world to see.

He did not vanish by a conjurer's trickery, nor was He banished by a royal decree. His departure was into the future of all believers who have the hope of His returning burning as a beacon in their hearts.

The same departure from the clutches of death that filled His adversaries' hearts with dread challenges each of us who believe to spend our lives in a manner that is worthy of His rising. We are confident that soon we too, from the trouble, toil, and tumult of a world waiting for its promised redemption, will be *gone*.

AFTERWORD

THIS INSPIRING BOOK, *Gone,* PUSHED my mind to consider those who have had to sit in a doctor's office waiting for their name to be called. Knowing the time of their appointment, they watch the clock as seconds seem like months and minutes seem like years. They replay every year of their lives, right up until this moment of their fragile existence, like a movie in their mind. They know this moment that is about to happen will change everything in their *now* and everything in their *not yet.* They have walked through the season of shock and unbelief of the reality that the dreams and desires they were looking forward to might only have been just that—dreams and desires, but never a reality.

As they wait, they remember the endless hours of prayer and the tireless efforts to get to every church service, standing in long prayer lines of people with needs of their own expecting a miracle from God. They have written every scripture they could find that confirms the God they serve is able to grant them the desires of their hearts and "by His stripes we are healed" (Isa. 53:5, NKJV). Since the first day they received the news that rocked their whole world, they've confessed every promise in the Bible from "no weapon formed against me will prosper" to "if God be for me who can be against me" (Isa. 54:17; Rom. 8:31). They have held on to every prophetic word written or spoken into their life. Yet reality reminds them that they are still human and that no one lives on this earth forever.

Their name is called, and now painful thoughts of death start warring with praise and thanks to God for life and life "more abundantly" (John 10:10, NKJV). What they have been waiting for has now arrived. The doctor walks in and slides the X-ray—proof—out of his folder and puts it under the glass in a dark place. Without hesitation he turns on the light—and miraculously what was once there is now *gone*.

Thank you, Dr. Rod Parsley, for giving us hope and reminding us every time that the same miracle that Mary, the mother of Jesus, experienced in her darkest hour of despair, standing at an empty tomb, is still available to us today.

Debt, depression, and despair—*gone*.

Pain, problems, and pressure—*gone*.

Trials, tribulation, and trouble—*gone*.

In this book you once again allowed God to use your pen to give not some but all the faith to believe that no matter what the enemy brings into our lives, we can stand on God's Word and without doubt declare, "It's *gone!*"

—BISHOP CLINT BROWN
FOUNDER AND PASTOR, JUDAH CHURCH

NOTES

INTRODUCTION

1. William Manchester, *American Caesar* (Boston: Little, Brown and Company, 1978), 271.

Chapter 1
THE JUBILEE OF THE UNIVERSE

1. Charles Noel Douglas, *Forty Thousand Quotations, Prose and Poetical* (London: George G. Harrap & Co. Ltd., 1917), 566.

2. As quoted in Charles Noel Douglas, ed., *Forty Thousand Sublime and Beautiful Thoughts Gathered from the Roses, Clover Blossoms, Geraniums, Violets, Morning-Glories, and Pansies of Literature* (New York: The Christian Herald, 1915), 280.

3. Rod Parsley, *God's End-Time Calendar* (Lake Mary, FL: Charisma House, 2015), 58; Pesahim 7:13.

4. Among the many sources drawn upon here, I am particularly indebted to Craig A. Evans of Acadia Divinity College and his study, "Jewish Burial Traditions and the Resurrection of Jesus," accessed December 27, 2015, http://craigaevans.com/Burial_Traditions.pdf.

5. Flavius Josephus, *The Antiquities of the Jews: Complete and Unabridged* 17, 8, 3, accessed December 29, 2015, http://www.documentacatholicaomnia.eu/03d/0037-0103

,_Flavius_Josephus,_The_Antiquities_Of_The_Jews ,_EN.pdf.

Chapter 2
INTO THE TOMB

1. Charles Haddon Spurgeon, *The Metropolitan Tabernacle Pulpit: Sermons Preached and Revised,* volume 24 (London: Passmore & Alabaster, 1879), 164.

2. Flavius Josephus, *Josephus in Nine Volumes: The Jewish War, Books IV–VII* (London: William Heinemann Ltd., 1961), 7, 1, 1.

3. Charles H. Spurgeon, *The Metropolitan Tabernacle Pulpit: Sermons Preached by C. H. Spurgeon,* volume 40 (London: Passmore & Alabaster, 1894), 582.

4. Spurgeon, *The Metropolitan Tabernacle Pulpit: Sermons Preached and Revised,* volume 24, 157.

Chapter 3
INTO HIDING

1. Andrew Murray, *God's Best Secrets* (New Kensington, PA: Whitaker House, 1999), 164.

2. This measure was derived from a creative reading of Joshua 3:4–5.

Chapter 4
INTO THE HEART OF THE EARTH

1. The word *catholic* as used here means "universal," as in the worldwide body of Christ.

2. John Calvin, *Calvin: Institutes of the Christian Religion, Volume 2,* John T. McNeill, ed. (Louisville, KY: Westminster John Knox Press, 1599), 16.8–12.

3. Martin Luther, "Von Jesu Christo eine Predigt zu Hofe zu Torgau gepredgt," April 16, 17, 1533. WA 37 (XXI) 35–72.

4. Charles Spurgeon, "Christ with the Keys of Death and Hell: Sermon No. 894" (sermon delivered at the Metropolitan Tabernacle Pulpit, Newington, London, England, October 3, 1869), accessed December 27, 2015, http://www.spurgeongems.org/vols13-15/chs894.pdf.

5. "Good Question: Did Jesus Really Descend to Hell?" *Christianity Today*, February 7, 2007, http://www.christianitytoday.com/ct/2000/february7/31.74.html.

6. Charles H. Spurgeon, *Spurgeon's Sermons on the Death and Resurrection of Jesus* (Peabody, MA: Hendrickson Publishers, 2005), 312.

7. Rod Parsley, *The Cross: One Man… One Tree… One Friday…* (Lake Mary, FL: Charisma House, 2013), 90–91.

8. "There Is a Fountain Filled With Blood" by William Cowper. 1772. Public domain.

Chapter 5
GRAVEYARD PLANET

1. As quoted in Douglas, *Forty Thousand Quotations*, 566.

2. As The Jewish Encyclopedia explains: "In Jewish communal life part of a day is at times reckoned as one day; e.g., the day of the funeral, even when the latter takes place late in the afternoon, is counted as the first of the seven days of mourning; a short time in the morning of the seventh day is counted as the seventh day; circumcision takes place on the eighth day, even though of the first day only a few minutes remained after the birth of the child, these being counted as one day." Isidore Singer and Cyrus Adler, eds., *The Jewish Encyclopedia: A Descriptive Record of the History, Religion, Literature,*

and Customs of the Jewish People from the Earliest Times to the Present Day, Volume 4, s.v. "Day" (New York: Funk & Wagnalls Company, 1901), 475.

3. Ron Rhodes, *1001 Unforgettable Quotes About God, Faith, and the Bible* (Eugene, OR: Harvest House, 2011), 201.

Chapter 6
HE IS NOT HERE

1. Phillips Brooks, *Christmas Songs and Easter Carols* (New York: E. P. Dutton & Co., 1903). Public domain.

2. Augustine of Hippo, *The Works of Aurelius Augustine: The Sermon on the Mount Expounded and The Harmony of the Evangelists, Volume 8*, Marcus Dods, ed. (Edinburgh: T. & T. Clark, 1873).

3. G. Campbell Morgan, *The Crises of the Christ* (New York: Fleming H. Revell Company, 1903), 364.

Chapter 7
BELIEVING

1. Albert Mohler, "The Resurrection of Jesus Christ and the Reality of the Gospel," Christianity.com, accessed December 27, 2015, http://www.christianity.com/bible /prophecy/the-resurrection-of-jesus-christ-and-the-reality -of-the-gospel-1320263.html.

2. Charles Colson, *Kingdoms in Conflict* (Grand Rapids, MI: Zondervan, 1987), 70.

3. Albert Mohler, "The Empty Tomb and the Risen Christ— The Centrality of the Resurrection to the Christian Faith," AlbertMohler.com, April 4, 2015, accessed December 27, 2015, http://www.albertmohler.com/2015 /04/04/the-empty-tomb-and-the-risen-christ-the -centrality-of-the-resurrection-to-the-christian-faith/.

4. James Bissett Pratt, *The Psychology of Religious Belief* (London: The Macmillan Company, 1908), 183.

5. As quoted in Carl McIntire, *Servants of Apostasy* (White-fish, MT: Kessinger Publishing, LLC, 2009), 248; see also Gladys Titzck Rhoads and Nancy Titzck Anderson, *McIntire: Defender of Faith and Freedom* (Maitland, FL: Xulon Press, 2012), 132.

6. Letter to the editor, *The Unitarian Register* 95, no. 28 (Boston: Christian Register Association, 1916), 657.

7. Charles H. Spurgeon, *Spurgeon's Sermons on the Death and Resurrection of Jesus* (Peabody, MA: Hendrickson Publishers, 2005), 585–86.

8. BrainyQuote.com, "Louis L'Amour Quotes," accessed December 27, 2015, http://www.brainyquote.com/quotes /quotes/l/louislamo386351.html.

Chapter 8
LIVING IN RESURRECTION POWER

1. Spurgeon, *Spurgeon's Sermons on the Death and Resurrection of Jesus*, 550.

Chapter 9
OVER THE HORIZON

1. Martin H. Manser, *The Westminster Collection Of Christian Quotations* (Louisville, KY: Westminster John Knox Press, 2001), 320.

2. Gary Thomas, "Atheism," *Christianity Today* 38, no. 11 (October 3, 1994): 26.

3. Richard Dawkins, "Richard Dawkins: You Ask the Questions Special," *The Independent*, December 3, 2006, http:// www.independent.co.uk/news/people/profiles/richard -dawkins-you-ask-the-questions-special-427003.html.